D0893904

TOLSTOY

TOLSTOY

BY

ROMAIN ROLLAND

TRANSLATED BY
BERNARD MIALL

WITHDRAWN

LIBRARY
MOUNT ST. MARY'S
COLLEGE
EMMITSBURG, MARYLAND

KENNIKAT PRESS
Port Washington, N. Y./London

TOLSTOY

First published in 1911
Reissued in 1972 by Kennikat Press
Library of Congress Catalog Card No: 74-160776
ISBN 0-8046-1608-6

Manufactured by Taylor Publishing Company   Dallas, Texas

PREFACE

To those of my own generation, the light that has but lately failed was the purest that illumined their youth. In the gloomy twilight of the later nineteenth century it shone as a star of consolation, whose radiance attracted and appeased our awakening spirits. As one of the many—for there are many in France—to whom Tolstoy was very much more than an admired artist : for whom he was a friend, the best of friends, the one true friend in the whole of European art—I wish to lay before this sacred memory my tribute of gratitude and of love.

The days when I learned to know him are days that I shall never forget. It was in 1886. After some years of silent germination the marvellous flowers of Russian art began to blossom on the soil of France. Translations of Tolstoy and of Dostoyevsky were being issued in feverish haste by all the publishing houses of Paris. Between the years '85 and '87 came *War and Peace, Anna Karenin, Childhood and Youth, Polikushka, The Death of Ivan Ilyitch*, the novels of the Caucasus, and the *Tales for the People*. In the space of a few months, almost of a few weeks, there was revealed to our eager eyes the presentment of a vast, unfamiliar life, in which was reflected a new people, a new world.

I had but newly entered the Normal College. My fellow-scholars were of widely divergent opinions. In our little world were such realistic and ironical spirits as the philosopher Georges Dumas; poets, like Suarès, burning with love of the Italian Renaissance; faithful disciples of classic tradition; Stendhalians, Wagnerians, atheists and mystics. It was a world of plentiful discussion, plentiful disagreement; but for a period of some months we were nearly all united by a common love of Tolstoy. It is true that each loved him for different reasons, for each discovered in him himself; but this love was a love that opened the door to a revelation of life; to the wide world itself. On every side—in our families, in our country homes—this mighty voice, which spoke from the confines of Europe, awakened the same emotions, unexpected as they often were. I remember my amazement upon hearing some middle-class people of Nivernais, my native province—people who felt no interest whatever in art, people who read practically nothing—speak with the most intense feeling of *The Death of Ivan Ilyitch*.

I have read, in the writings of distinguished critics, the theory that Tolstoy owed the best of his ideas to the French romantics: to George Sand, to Victor Hugo. We may ignore the absurdity of supposing that Tolstoy, who could not endure her, could ever have been subject

to the influence of George Sand ; but we cannot
deny the influence of Jean-Jacques Rousseau and
of Stendhal ; nevertheless, we belittle the greatness
of Tolstoy, and the power of his fascination, if
we attribute them to his ideas. The circle of
ideas in which art moves and has its being is a
narrow one. It is not in those ideas that his
might resides, but in his expression of them ;
in the personal accent, the imprint of the artist,
the colour and savour of his life.

Whether Tolstoy's ideas were or were not
borrowed—a matter to be presently considered—
never yet had a voice like to his resounded throughout Europe. How else can we explain the thrill of
emotion which we all of us felt upon hearing that
psychic music, that harmony for which we had so
long waited, and of which we felt the need ? In our
opinion the style counted for nothing. Most of us,
myself included, made the acquaintance of Melchior
de Vogüé's work on the subject of the Russian
novel [1] after we had read the novels of Tolstoy ;
and his admiration of our hero seemed, after ours,
a pallid thing. M. de Vogüé spoke essentially as a
man of letters pure and simple. But for our part it
was not enough to admire the presentation of life :
we lived it ; it was our own. Ours it was by its
ardent love of life, by its quality of youth ; ours by
its irony, its disillusion, its pitiless discernment, and
its haunting sense of mortality. Ours by its dreams
of brotherly love, of peace among men ; ours by its
terrible accusation of the lies of civilisation ; ours

[1] *Le Roman russe.*

by its realism ; by its mysticism ours ; by its savour
of nature, its sense of invisible forces, its vertigo in
the face of the infinite.

To many of us the novels of Tolstoy were what
Werther was to an earlier generation : the wonderful
mirror of our passions, our strength, our weak-
nesses, of our hopes, our terrors, our discourage-
ment. We were in no wise anxious to reconcile
these many contradictions ; still less did we con-
cern ourselves to imprison this complex, multiple
mind, full of echoes of the whole wide world,
within the narrow limits of religious or political
categories, as have the greater number of those
who have written of Tolstoy in these latter years :
incapable of extricating themselves from the conflict of parties, dragging him into the arena of their
own passions, measuring him by the standards of
their socialistic or clerical coteries. As if our
coteries could be the measure of a genius ! What
is it to me if Tolstoy is or is not of my party ?
Shall I ask of what party Shakespeare was, or Dante,
before I breathe the atmosphere of his magic or
steep myself in its light ?

We did not say, as do the critics of to-day, that
there were two Tolstoys : the Tolstoy of the period
before the crisis and he of the period after the
crisis ; that the one was the great artist, while the
other was not an artist at all. For us there was
only one Tolstoy, and we loved the whole of him ;
for we felt, instinctively, that in such souls as his all
things are bound together and each has its integral
place.

CONTENTS

PAGE

PREFACE 5

CHAPTER

I. CHILDHOOD 11

II. BOYHOOD AND YOUTH 21

III. YOUTH : THE ARMY . . . 31

IV. EARLY WORK : TALES OF THE CAUCASUS . 37

V. SEBASTOPOL : WAR AND RELIGION . . 47

VI. ST. PETERSBURG 59

VII. "FAMILY HAPPINESS" . . . 73

VIII. MARRIAGE 81

IX. "ANNA KARENIN" . . . 97

X. THE CRISIS 109

XI. REALITY 125

10   **CONTENTS**

CHAPTER		PAGE
XII.	ART AND CONSCIENCE	133
XIII.	SCIENCE AND ART	143
XIV.	THEORIES OF ART : MUSIC . . .	163
XV.	"RESURRECTION"	185
XVI.	RELIGION AND POLITICS . . .	197
XVII.	OLD AGE	217
XVIII.	CONCLUSION	235
	INDEX	249

I

CHILDHOOD

TOLSTOY

CHAPTER I

CHILDHOOD

OUR instinct was conscious then of that which reason must prove to-day. The task is possible now, for the long life has attained its term; revealing itself, unveiled, to the eyes of all, with unequalled candour, unexampled sincerity. To-day we are at once arrested by the degree in which that life has always remained the same, from the beginning to the end, in spite of all the barriers which critics have sought to erect here and there along its course ; in spite of Tolstoy himself, who, like every impassioned mind, was inclined to the belief, when he loved, or conceived a faith, that he loved or believed for the first time ; that the commencement of his true life dated from that moment. Commencement—recommencement ! How often his mind was the theatre of the same struggles, the same crises ! We cannot speak of the unity of his ideas, for no such unity existed ; we can only speak of the persistence among them of the same diverse elements ; sometimes allied, sometimes inimical ; more often enemies than allies. Unity is to be found neither in the spirit nor the mind of a Tolstoy ; it exists only in the internal conflict of his passions, in the tragedy of his art and his life.

In him life and art are one. Never was work more intimately mingled with the artist's life ; it has, almost constantly, the value of autobiography ; it enables us to follow the writer, step by step, from the time when he was twenty-five years of age, throughout all the contradictory experiences of his adventurous career. His *Journal*, which he commenced before the completion of his twentieth year, and continued until his death,[1] together with the notes furnished by M. Birukov,[2] completes this knowledge, and enable us not only to read almost day by day in the history of Tolstoy's conscience, but also to reconstitute the world in which his genius struck root, and the minds from which his own drew sustenance.

His was a rich inheritance. The Tolstoys and the Volkonskys were very ancient families, of the greater nobility, claiming descent from Rurik ; numbering among their ancestors companions of Peter the Great, generals of the Seven Years' War,

[1] With the exception of a few interruptions : one especially of considerable length, between 1865 and 1878.

[2] For his remarkable biography of *Léon Tolstoï, Vie et Œuvre, Mémoires, Souvenirs, Lettres, Extraits du Journal intime, Notes et Documents biographiques, réunis, coordonnés et annotés par P. Birukov*, revised by Leo Tolstoy, translated into French from the MS. by J. W. Bienstock.

heroes of the Napoleonic struggle, Decembrists, and political exiles. This inheritance included family traditions ; old memories to which Tolstoy was indebted for some of the most original types in his *War and Peace ;* there was the old Prince Bolkonsky, his maternal grandfather, Voltairian, despotic, a belated representative of the aristocracy of the days of Catherine II.; Prince Nikolas Grigorovitch Volkonsky, a cousin of his mother, who was wounded at Austerlitz, and, like Prince Andrei, was carried off the field of battle under the eyes of Napoleon ; his father, who had some of the characteristics of Nicolas Rostoff ;[1] and his mother, the Princess Marie, the ugly, charming woman with the beautiful eyes, whose goodness illumines the pages of *War and Peace.*

He scarcely knew his parents. Those delightful narratives, *Childhood* and *Youth,* have, therefore, but little authenticity ; for the writer's mother died when he was not yet two years of age. He, therefore, was unable to recall the beloved face which the little Nikolas Irtenieff evoked beyond a veil of tears : a face with a luminous smile, which radiated gladness. . . .

"Ah ! if in difficult moments I could only see that smile, I should not know what sorrow is."[2]

Yet she doubtless endowed him with her own absolute candour, her indifference to opinion, and

---

[1] He also fought in the Napoleonic campaigns, and was a prisoner in France during the years 1814–15.

[2] *Childhood,* chap. ii.

her wonderful gift of relating tales of her own invention.

His father he did in some degree remember. His was a genial yet ironical spirit ; a sad-eyed man who dwelt upon his estates, leading an independent, unambitious life. Tolstoy was nine years old when he lost him. His death caused him "for the first time to understand the bitter truth, and filled his soul with despair." [1] Here was the child's earliest encounter with the spectre of terror ; and henceforth a portion of his life was to be devoted to fighting the phantom, and a portion to its celebration, its transfiguration. The traces of this agony are marked by a few unforgettable touches in the final chapters of his *Childhood*, where his memories are transposed in the narrative of the death and burial of his mother.

Five children were left orphans in the old house at Yasnaya Polyana.[2] There Leo Nikolayevitch was born, on the 28th of August, 1828, and there, eighty-two years later, he was to die. The youngest of the five was a girl : that Marie who in later years

---

[1] *Childhood*, chap. xxvii.

[2] Yasnaya Polyana, the name of which signifies " the open glade" (literally, the "light glade"), is a little village to the south of Moscow, at a distance of some leagues from Toula, in one of the most thoroughly Russian of the provinces. "Here the two great regions of Russia," says M. Leroy-Beaulieu, "the region of the forests and the agricultural region, meet and melt into each other. In the surrounding country we meet with no Finns, Tatars, Poles, Jews, or Little Russians. The district of Toula lies at the very heart of Russia."

became a religious; it was with her that Tolstoy took refuge in dying, when he fled from home and family. Of the four sons, Sergius was charming and selfish, "sincere to a degree that I have never known equalled"; Dmitri was passionate, self-centred, introspective, and in later years, as a student, abandoned himself eagerly to the practices of religion; caring nothing for public opinion; fasting, seeking out the poor, sheltering the infirm; suddenly, with the same quality of violence, plunging into debauchery; then, tormented by remorse, ransoming a girl whom he had known in a public brothel, and receiving her into his home; finally dying of phthisis at the age of twenty-nine.[1] Nikolas, the eldest, the favourite brother, had inherited his mother's gift of imagination, her power of telling stories;[2] ironical, nervous, and refined; in later years an officer in the Caucasus, where he formed the habit of a drunkard; a man, like his brother, full of Christian kindness, living in hovels, and sharing with the poor all that he possessed. Tourgenev said of him "that he put into practice that humble attitude towards life which his brother Leo was content to develop in theory."

The orphans were cared for by two great-hearted women, one was their Aunt Tatiana,[3] of whom Tolstoy said that "she had two virtues: serenity

[1] Tolstoy has depicted him in *Anna Karenin*, as the brother of Levine.

[2] He wrote the *Diary of a Hunter*.

[3] In reality she was a distant relative. She had loved Tolstoy's father, and was loved by him; but effaced herself, like Sonia in *War and Peace*.

and love." Her whole life was love; a devotion
that never failed. "She made me understand the
moral pleasure of loving."

The other was their Aunt Alexandra, who was
for ever serving others, herself avoiding service,
dispensing with the help of servants. Her favourite
occupation was reading the lives of the Saints, or
conversing with pilgrims or the feeble-minded. Of
these "innocents" there were several, men and
women, who lived in the house. One, an old
woman, a pilgrim, was the godmother of Tolstoy's
sister. Another, the idiot Gricha, knew only how
to weep and pray. . . .

"Gricha, notable Christian ! So mighty was your
faith that you felt the approach of God; so ardent
was your love that words rushed from your lips,
words that your reason could not control. And
how you used to celebrate His splendour, when
speech failed you, when, all tears, you lay prostrated
on the ground !" [1]

Who can fail to understand the influence, in the
shaping of Tolstoy, of all these humble souls ? In
some of them we seem to see an outline, a prophecy,
of the Tolstoy of later years. Their prayers and
their affection must have sown the seeds of faith
in the child's mind ; seeds of which the aged man
was to reap the harvest.

With the exception of the idiot Gricha, Tolstoy
does not speak, in his narrative of *Childhood*, of
these humble helpers who assisted in the work of
building up his mind. But then how clearly we

[1] *Childhood*, chap. xii.

see it through the medium of the book—this soul
of a little child; "this pure, loving heart, a ray of
clear light, which always discovered in others the
best of their qualities"—this more than common
tenderness! Being happy, he ponders on the only
creature he knows to be unhappy; he cries at the
thought, and longs to devote himself to his good.
He hugs and kisses an ancient horse, begging his
pardon, because he has hurt him. He is happy in
loving, even if he is not loved. Already we can see
the germs of his future genius; his imagination, so
vivid that he cries over his own stories; his brain,
always busy, always trying to discover of what other
people think; his precocious powers of memory [1]
and observation; the attentive eyes, which even in
the midst of his sorrow scrutinise the faces about
him, and the authenticity of their sorrow. He tells
us that at five years of age he felt for the first time
"that life is not a time of amusement, but a very
heavy task." [2]

Happily he forgot the discovery. In those days
he used to soothe his mind with popular tales;
those mythical and legendary dreams known in
Russia as *bylines;* stories from the Bible; above
all the sublime *History of Joseph*, which he cited in
his old age as a model of narrative art: and, finally,
the Arabian Nights, which at his grandmother's
house were recited every evening, from the vantage
of the window-seat, by a blind story-teller.

[1] He professes, in his autobiographical notes (dated 1878),
to be able to recall the sensations of being swaddled as a baby,
and of being bathed in a tub. See *First Memories.*

[2] *First Memories.*

II

BOYHOOD
AND
YOUTH

CHAPTER II

BOYHOOD AND YOUTH

HE studied at Kazan.[1] He was not a notable student. It used to be said of the three brothers [2] : "Sergius wants to, and can ; Dmitri wants to, and can't ; Leo can't, and doesn't want to."

He passed through the period which he terms "the desert of adolescence" ; a desert of sterile sands, blown upon by gales of the burning winds of folly. The pages of *Boyhood,* and in especial those of *Youth,*[3] are rich in intimate confessions relating to these years.

He was a solitary. His brain was in a condition

[1] From 1842 to 1847. [Science was as yet unorganised ; and its teachers, even in Western Europe, had not the courage of the facts they taught. Men still sought for an anchor in the philosophic systems of the ancients. The theory of evolution, put forward at the beginning of the century, had fallen into obscurity. Science was dry, dogmatic, uncoordinated, insignificant. Hence, perhaps, the contempt for science which distinguised Tolstoy throughout his life, and which made the later Tolstoy possible.—TRANS.]

[2] Nikolas, five years older than Leo, had completed his studies in 1844.

[3] The English translation is entitled *Childhood, Boyhood, Youth.*

of perpetual fever. For a year he was completely at sea ; he roamed from one system of philosophy to another. As a Stoic, he indulged in self-inflicted physical tortures. As an Epicurean he debauched himself. Then came a faith in metempsychosis. Finally he fell into a condition of nihilism not far removed from insanity ; he used to feel that if only he could turn round with sufficient rapidity he would find himself face to face with nothingness . . . He analysed himself continually :

" I no longer thought of a thing ; I thought of what I thought of it."[1]

This perpetual self-analysis, this mechanism of reason turning in the void, remained to him as a dangerous habit, which was " often," in his own words, "to be detrimental to me in life" ; but by which his art has profited inexpressibly.[2]

As another result of self-analysis, he had lost all his religious convictions ; or such was his belief. At sixteen years of age ceased to pray ; he went to church no longer ;[3] but his faith was not extinguished ; it was only smouldering.

" Nevertheless, I did believe—in something. But in what ? I could not say. I still believed in God ; or rather I did not deny Him. But in what God ? I did not know. Nor did I deny Christ and his teaching ; but I could not have said precisely what that doctrine was."[4]

---

[1] *Youth*, xix.

[2] Notably in his first volumes—in the *Tales of Sebastopol*.

[3] This was the time when he used to read Voltaire, and find pleasure in so doing.   [4] *Confessions*, vol. i.

From time to time he was obsessed by dreams of goodness. He wished to sell his carriage and give the money to the poor : to give them the tenth part of his fortune; to live without the help of servants, " for they were men like himself." During an illness[1] he wrote certain " Rules of Life." He naïvely assigned himself the duty of " studying everything, of mastering all subjects : law, medicine, languages, agriculture, history, geography, and mathematics ; to attain the highest degree of perfection in music and painting," and so forth. He had " the conviction that the destiny of man was a process of incessant self-perfection."

Insensibly, under the stress of a boy's passions, of a violent sensuality and a stupendous pride of self,[2] this faith in perfection went astray, losing its disinterested quality, becoming material and practical. If he still wished to perfect his will, his body, and his mind, it was in order to conquer the world and to enforce its love.[3] He wished to please.

To please : it was not an easy ambition. He was then of a simian ugliness : the face was long, heavy,

---

[1] In March and April, 1847.

[2] " All that man does he does out of *amour-propre*," says Nekhludov, in *Boyhood*.

In 1853 Tolstoy writes, in his *Journal:* " My great failing : pride. A vast self-love, without justification. . . . I am so ambitious that if I had to choose between glory and virtue (which I love) I am sure I should choose the former."

[3] " I wanted to be known by all, loved by all. I wanted every one, at the mere sound of my name, to be struck with admiration and gratitude."

LIBRARY
OF
MOUNT ST. MARY'S
COLLEGE
EMMITSBURG, MARYLAND

brutish ; the hair was cropped close, growing low upon the forehead ; the eyes were small, with a hard, forbidding glance, deeply sunken in shadowy orbits ; the nose was large, the lips were thick and protruding, and the ears were enormous.[1]   Unable to alter this ugliness, which even as a child had subjected him to fits of despair,[2] he pretended to a realisation of the ideal man of the world, *l'homme comme il faut*.[3]   This ideal led him to do as did other " men of the world " : to gamble, run foolishly into debt, and to live a completely dissipated exist‑ence.[4]

One quality always came to his salvation : his absolute sincerity.

" Do you know why I like you better than the others ? " says Nekhludov to his friend.   " You have a precious and surprising quality : candour."

" Yes, I am always saying things which I am ashamed to own even to myself."[5]

In his wildest moments he judges himself with a pitiless insight.

[1] According to a portrait dated 1848, in which year he attained his twentieth year.

[2] " I thought there would be no happiness on earth for any one who had so large a nose, so thick lips, and such small eyes."

[3] " I divided humanity into three classes : the ' correct,' or ' smart,' who alone were worthy of esteem ; those who were not ' correct,' who deserved only contempt and hatred ; and the people, the *plebs*, who simply did not exist." (*Youth*, xxxi.)

[4] Especially during a period spent in St. Petersburg, 1847–48.

[5] *Boyhood*.

" I am living an utterly bestial life," he writes in his *Journal*. " I am as low as one can fall." Then, with his mania for analysis, he notes minutely the causes of his errors :

" 1. Indecision or lack of energy. 2. Self-deception. 3. Insolence. 4. False modesty. 5. Illtemper. 6. Licentiousness. 7. Spirit of imitation. 8. Versatility. 9. Lack of reflection."

While still a student he was applying this independence of judgment to the criticism of social conventions and intellectual superstitions. He scoffed at the official science of the University ; denied the least importance to historical studies, and was put under arrest for his audacity of thought. At this period he discovered Rousseau, reading his *Confessions* and *Émile*. The discovery affected him like a mental thunderbolt.

"I made him an object of religious worship. I wore a medallion portrait of him hung round my neck, as though it were a holy image." [1]

His first essays in philosophy took the form of commentaries on Rousseau (1846–47).

In the end, however, disgusted with the University and with " smartness," he returned to Yasnaya Polyana, to bury himself in the country (1847–51) ; where he once more came into touch with the people. He professed to come to their assistance, as their benefactor and their teacher. His experiences of this period have been related in one of his earliest books, *A Russian Proprietor* (*A Landlord's*

[1] Conversations with M. Paul Boyer (*Le Temps*), August 28, 1901.

Morning) (1852) ; a remarkable novel, whose hero,
Prince Nekhludov,[1] is Tolstoy in disguise.

Nekhludov is twenty years old. He has left the
University to devote himself to his peasants. He
has been labouring for a year to do them good.
In the course of a visit to the village we see him
striving against jeering indifference, rooted distrust,
routine, apathy, vice, and ingratitude. All his
efforts are in vain. He returns indoors discouraged,
and muses on his dreams of a year ago ; his
generous enthusiasm, his " idea that love and goodness were one with happiness and truth : the only
happiness and the only truth possible in this world."
He feels himself defeated. He is weary and
ashamed.

" Seated before the piano, his hand unconsciously
moved upon the keys. A chord sounded ; then
a second, then a third. . . . He began to play.
The chords were not always perfect in rhythm ;
they were often obvious to the point of banality ;
they did not reveal any talent for music ; but they
gave him a melancholy, indefinable sense of pleasure. At each change of key he awaited, with a
flutter of the heart, for what was about to follow ;

---

[1] Nekhludov figures also in *Boyhood* and *Youth* (1854), in *A
Brush with the Enemy* (1856) ; the *Diary of a Sportsman* (1856) ;
Lucerne (1857) ; and *Resurrection* (1899). We must remember
that different characters appear under this one name.
Tolstoy has not always given Nekhludov the same physical
aspect ; and the latter commits suicide at the end of the
Diary of a Sportsman. These different Nekhludovs are various
aspects of Tolstoy, endowed with his worst and his best
characteristics.

his imagination vaguely supplementing the deficiencies of the actual sound. He heard a choir, an orchestra . . . and his keenest pleasure arose from the enforced activity of his imagination, which brought before him, without logical connection, but with astonishing clearness, the most varied scenes and images of the past and the future. . . ."

Once more he sees the moujiks—vicious, distrustful, lying, idle, obstinate, contrary, with whom he has lately been speaking ; but this time he sees them with all their good qualities and without their vices ; he sees into their hearts with the intuition of love ; he sees therein their patience, their resignation to the fate which is crushing them ; their forgiveness of wrongs, their family affection, and the causes of their pious, mechanical attachment to the past. He recalls their days of honest labour, healthy and fatiguing. . . .

"'It is beautiful,' he murmurs . . . 'Why am I not one of these ?'" [1]

The entire Tolstoy is already contained in the hero of this first novel ; [2] his piercing vision and his persistent illusions. He observes men and women with an impeccable realism ; but no sooner does he close his eyes than his dreams resume their sway ; his dreams and his love of mankind.

---

[1] *A Russian Proprietor.*
[2] Contemporary with *Childhood.*

III

YOUTH:
THE ARMY

CHAPTER III

YOUTH : THE ARMY

TOLSTOY, in the year 1850, was not as patient as Nekhludov. Yasnaya Polyana had disillusioned and disappointed him. He was as weary of the people as he was of the world of fashion; his attitude as benefactor wearied him; he could bear it no more. Moreover, he was harassed by creditors. In 1851 he escaped to the Caucasus; to the army in which his brother Nikolas was already an officer.

He had hardly arrived, hardly tasted the quiet of the mountains, before he was once more master of himself; before he had recovered his God.

"Last night[1] I hardly slept. I began to pray to God. I cannot possibly express the sweetness of the feeling that came to me when I prayed. I recited the customary prayers; but I went on praying for a long time. I felt the desire of something very great, very beautiful. . . . What? I cannot say what. I wanted to be one with the Infinite Being: to be dissolved, comprehended, in Him. I begged Him to forgive me my trespasses. . . .

---

[1] The 11th of June, 1851, in the fortified camp of Starï-Iourt, in the Caucasus.

But no, I did not beg Him; I felt that He did pardon me, since He granted me that moment of wonderful joy. I was praying, yet at the same time I felt that I could not, dared not pray. I thanked Him, not in words, but in thought. . . . Scarcely an hour had passed, and I was listening to the voice of vice. I fell asleep dreaming of glory, of women : it was stronger than I. Never mind ! I thank God for that moment of happiness : for showing me my pettiness and my greatness. I want to pray, but I do not know how ; I want to understand, but I dare not. I abandon myself to Thy will !" [1]

The flesh was not conquered ; not then, nor ever ; the struggle between God and the passions of man continued in the silence of his heart. Tolstoy speaks in his *Journal* of the three demons which were devouring him :

1. *The passion for gambling.* Possible struggle.
2. *Sensuality.* Struggle very difficult.
3. *Vanity.* The most terrible of all.

At the very moment when he was dreaming of living for others and of sacrificing himself, voluptuous or futile thoughts would assail him : the image of some Cossack woman, or "the despair he would feel if his moustache were higher on one side than the other."—"No matter !" God was there ; He would not forsake him. Even the effervescence of the struggle was fruitful : all the forces of life were exalted thereby.

"I think the idea of making a journey to the

[1] *Journal.*

Caucasus, however frivolous at the time of conception, was inspired in me from above. God's hand has guided me. I never cease to thank Him. I feel that I have become better here ; and I am firmly convinced that whatever happens to me can only be for my good, since it is God Himself who has wished it. . . ." [1]

It is the song of gratitude of the earth in spring. Earth covers herself with flowers ; all is well, all is beautiful. In 1852 the genius of Tolstoy produces its earliest flowers : *Childhood, The Russian Proprietor, The Invasion, Boyhood ;* and he thanks the Spirit of life who has made him fruitful.[2]

---

[1] Letter to his Aunt Tatiana, January, 1852.

[2] A portrait dated 1851 already shows the change which is being accomplished in his mind. The head is raised ; the expression is somewhat brighter ; the cavities of the orbits are less in shadow ; the eyes themselves still retain their fixed severity of look, and the open mouth, shadowed by a growing moustache, is gloomy and sullen ; there is still a quality of defiant pride, but far more youth.

IV

EARLY WORK:
TALES OF
THE CAUCASUS

CHAPTER IV

EARLY WORK : TALES OF THE CAUCASUS

The Story of my Childhood [1] was commenced in
the autumn of 1851, at Tiflis ; it was finished at
Piatigorsk in the Caucasus, on the 2nd of July, 1852.
It is curious to note that while in the midst of that
nature by which he was so intoxicated, while leading
a life absolutely novel, in the midst of the stirring
risks of warfare, occupied in the discovery of a
world of unfamiliar characters and passions, Tolstoy
should have returned, in this his first work, to
the memories of his past life. But *Childhood* was
written during a period of illness, when his military
activity was suddenly arrested. During the long
leisure of a convalescence, while alone and suffering,
his state of mind inclined to the sentimental ; [2] the
past unrolled itself before his eyes at a time when he
felt for it a certain tenderness. After the exhausting tension of the last few unprofitable years,
it was comforting to live again in thought the

---

[1] Published in English as part of *Childhood, Boyhood, Youth*.
[2] His letters of this period to his Aunt Tatiana are full of
tears and of sentimentality. He was, as he says, *Liova-riova*,
" Leo the Sniveller " (January 6, 1852).

"marvellous, innocent, joyous, poetic period" of early childhood ; to reconstruct for himself "the heart of a child, good, sensitive, and capable of love." With the ardour of youth and its illimitable projects, with the cyclic character of his poetic imagination, which rarely conceived an isolated subject, and whose great romances are only the links in a long historic chain, the fragments of enormous conceptions which he was never able to execute,[1] Tolstoy at this moment regarded his narrative of *Childhood* as merely the opening chapters of a *History of Four Periods*, which was to include his life in the Caucasus, and was in all probability to have terminated in the revelation of God by Nature.

In later years Tolstoy spoke with great severity of his *Childhood*, to which he owed some part of his popularity.

"It is so bad," he remarked to M. Birukov : "it is written with so little literary conscience ! . . . There is nothing to be got from it."

He was alone in this opinion. The manuscript was sent, without the author's name, to the great Russian review, the *Sovremennik* (*Contemporary*) ; it was published immediately (September 6, 1852), and achieved a general success; a success confirmed by the public of every country in Europe. Yet in

---

[1] The *Russian Proprietor* (*A Landlord's Morning*) is the fragment of a projected *Romance of a Russian Landowner*. *The Cossacks* forms the first portion of a great romance of the Caucasus. In the author's eyes the huge *War and Peace* was only a sort of preface to a contemporary epic, of which *The Decembrists* was to have been the nucleus.

spite of its poetic charm, its delicacy of touch and emotion, we can understand that it may have displeased the Tolstoy of later years.

It displeased him for the very reasons by which it pleased others. We must admit it frankly : except in the recording of certain provincial types, and in a restricted number of passages which are remarkable for their religious feeling or for the realistic treatment of emotion,[1] the personality of Tolstoy is barely in evidence.

A tender, gentle sentimentality prevails from cover to cover ; a quality which was always afterwards antipathetic to Tolstoy, and one which he sedulously excluded from his other romances. We recognise it ; these tears, this sentimentality came from Dickens, who was one of Tolstoy's favourite authors between his fourteenth and his twenty-first year. Tolstoy notes in his *Journal :* "Dickens : *David Copperfield.* Influence considerable." He read the book again in the Caucasus.

Two other influences, to which he himself confesses, were Sterne and Töppfer. "I was then," he says, " under their inspiration."[2]

Who would have thought that the *Nouvelles Genevoises* would be the first model of the author of *War and Peace ?* Yet knowing this to be a fact, we discern in Tolstoy's *Childhood* the same bantering, affected geniality, transplanted to the soil of a more aristocratic nature. So we see that

---

[1] See the passage relating to the pilgrim Gricha, or to the death of his mother.

[2] Letter to Birukov.

the readers of his earliest efforts found the writer's countenance familiar. It was not long, however, before his own personality found self-expression. His *Boyhood* (*Adolescence*), though less pure and less perfect than *Childhood*, exhibits a more orginal power of psychology, a keen feeling for nature, and a mind full of distress and conflict, which Dickens or Töpffer would have been at a loss to express. In the *Russian Proprietor* (October, 1852 [1]) Tolstoy's character appeared sharply defined, marked by his fearless sincerity and his faith in love. Among the remarkable portraits of peasants which he has painted in this novel, we find an early sketch of one of the finest conceptions of his *Popular Tales* : the old man with the beehives ; [2] the little old man under the birch-tree, his hands outstretched, his eyes raised, his bald head shining in the sun, and all around him the bees, touched with gold, never stinging him, forming a halo. . . . But the truly typical works of this period are those which directly register his present emotions : namely, the novels of the Caucasus. The first, *The Invasion* (finished in December, 1852), impresses the reader deeply by the magnificence of its landscapes : a sunrise amidst the mountains, on the bank of a river ; a wonderful night-piece, with sounds and shadows noted with a striking intensity ; and the return in the evening, while the distant snowy peaks disappear in the violet haze, and the clear voices of the regimental singers rise and fall in the

[1] Completed only in 1855–56.
[2] *The Two Old Men* (1885).

transparent air.   Many of the types of *War and Peace* are here drawn to the life : Captain Khlopoff, the true hero, who by no means fights because he likes fighting, but because it is his duty ; a man with "one of those truly Russian faces, placid and simple, and eyes into which it is easy and agreeable to gaze."

Heavy, awkward, a trifle ridiculous, indifferent to his surroundings, he alone is unchanged in battle, where all the rest are changed ; "he is exactly as we have seen him always : with the same quiet movements, the same level voice, the same expression of simplicity on his heavy, simple face."   Next comes the lieutenant who   imitates the heroes of Lermontov ; a most kindly, affectionate boy, who professes the utmost ferocity. Then   comes the poor little subaltern, delighted at the idea of his first action, brimming over with affection, ready to fall on his comrade's neck ; a laughable, adorable boy, who, like Petia Rostoff, contrives to get stupidly killed.   In the centre of the picture is the figure of Tolstoy, the observer, who is mentally aloof from his comrades, and already utters his cry of protest against warfare :

"Is it impossible, then, for men to live in peace, in this world so full of beauty, under this immeasurable starry sky ?   How is it they are able, here, to retain their feelings of hostility and vengeance, and the lust of destroying their fellows ? All there is of evil in the human heart ought to disappear at the touch of nature, that most immediate expression of the beautiful and the good." [1]

[1] *The Invasion.*

Other tales of the Caucasus were to follow which were observed at this time, though not written until a later period. In 1854–55. *The Woodcutters* was written ; a book notable for its exact and rather frigid realism ; full of curious records of Russian soldier-psychology—notes to be made use of in the future. In 1856 appeared *A Brush with the Enemy,* in which there is a man of the world, a degraded non-commissioned officer, a wreck, a coward, a drunkard and a liar, who cannot support the idea of being slaughtered like one of the common soldiers he despises, the least of whom is worth a hundred of himself.

Above all these works, as the summit, so to speak, of this first mountain range, rises one of the most beautiful lyric romances that ever fell from Tolstoy's pen : the song of his youth, the poem of the Caucasus, *The Cossacks.*[1] The splendour of the snowy mountains displaying their noble lines against the luminous sky fills the whole work with its music. The book is unique, for it belongs to the flowering-time of genius, " the omnipotent god of youth," as Tolstoy says, " that rapture which never returns." What a spring-tide torrent ! What an overflow of love !

" ' I love—I love so much ! . . . How brave ! How good ! ' he repeated : and he felt as though he must weep. Why ? Who was brave, and whom did he love ? That he did not precisely know."[2]

---

[1] Although completed much later—in 1860—and appearing only in 1863—the bulk of this volume was of this period.

[2] *The Cossacks.*

This intoxication of the heart flows on, un-
checked. Olenin, the hero, who has come to
the Caucasus, as Tolstoy came, to steep himself in
nature, in the life of adventure, becomes enamoured
of a young Cossack girl, and abandons himself to
the medley of his contradictory aspirations. At
one moment he believes that "happiness is to
live for others, to sacrifice oneself," at another,
that "self-sacrifice is only stupidity"; finally he
is inclined to believe, with Erochta, the old Cossack,
that "everything is precious. God has made
everything for the delight of man. Nothing is
a sin. To amuse oneself with a handsome girl is
not a sin : it is only health." But what need to
think at all ? It is enough to live. Life is all good,
all happiness ; life is all-powerful and universal ;
life is God. An ardent naturalism uplifts and
consumes his soul. Lost in the forest, amidst
"the wildness of the woods, the multitude of
birds and animals, the clouds of midges in the
dusky green, in the warm, fragrant air, amidst the
little runlets of water which trickle everywhere
beneath the boughs"; a few paces from the
ambushes of the enemy, Olenin is "seized suddenly by such a sense of causeless happiness that
in obedience to childish habit he crossed himself
and began to give thanks to somebody." Like a
Hindu fakir, he rejoices to tell himself that he is
alone and lost in this maëlstrom of aspiring life :
that myriads of invisible beings, hidden on every
hand, are that moment hunting him to death ;
that these thousands of little insects humming
around him are calling :

"'Here, brothers, here! Here is some one to bite!'"

And it became obvious to him that he was no longer a Russian gentleman, in Moscow society, but simply a creature like the midge, the pheasant, the stag : like those which were living and prowling about him at that moment.

" Like them, I shall live, I shall die. And the grass will grow above me. . . ."

And his heart is full of happiness.

Tolstoy lives through this hour of youth in a delirium of vitality and the love of life. He embraces Nature, and sinks himself in her being. To her he pours forth and exalts his griefs, his joys, and his loves; in her he lulls them to sleep. Yet this romantic intoxication never veils the lucidity of his perceptions. Nowhere has he painted landscape with a greater power than in this fervent poem ; nowhere has he depicted the type with greater truth. The contrast of nature with the world of men, which forms the basis of the book; and which through all Tolstoy's life is to prove one of his favourite themes, and an article of his *Credo*, has already inspired him, the better to castigate the world, with something of the bitterness to be heard in the *Kreutzer Sonata*.[1] But for those who love him he is no less truly himself ; and the creatures of nature, the beautiful Cossack girl and her friends, are seen under a searching light, with their egoism, their cupidity, their venality, and all their vices.

An exceptional occasion was about to offer itself for the exercise of this heroic veracity.

[1] For example, see Oleniln's letter to his friends in Russia.

V

SEBASTOPOL:
WAR AND
RELIGION

CHAPTER V

In November, 1853, war was declared upon Turkey. Tolstoy obtained an appointment to the army of Roumania ; he was transferred to the army of the Crimea, and on November 7, 1854, he arrived in Sebastopol. He was burning with enthusiasm and patriotic faith. He went about his duties courageously, and was often in danger, in especial throughout the April and May of 1855, when he served on every alternate day in the battery of of the 4th bastion.

Living for months in a perpetual tremor and exaltation, face to face with death, his religious mysticism revived. He became familiar with God. In April, 1855, he noted in his diary a prayer to God, thanking Him for His protection in danger and beseeching Him to continue it, "so that I may achieve the glorious and eternal end of life, of which I am still ignorant, although I feel a presentiment of it." Already this object of his life was not art, but religion. On March 5, 1855, he wrote :

"I have been led to conceive a great idea, to

whose realisation I feel capable of devoting my whole life. This idea is the foundation of a new religion ; the religion of the Christ, but purified of dogmas and mysteries. . . . To act with a clear conscience, in order to unite men by means of religion." [1]

This was to be the programme of his old age.

However, to distract himself from the spectacles which surrounded him, he began once more to write. How could he, amidst that hail of lead, find the necessary freedom of mind for the writing of the third part of his memories : *Youth ?* The book is chaotic ; and we may attribute to the conditions of its production a quality of disorder, and at times a certain dryness of abstract analysis, which is increased by divisions and subdivisions after the manner of Stendhal.[2] Yet we admire his calm penetration of the mist of dreams and inchoate ideas which crowd a young brain. His work is extraordinarily true to itself, and at moments what poetic freshness !—as in the vivid picture of springtime in the city, or the tale of the confession, and the journey to the convent, on

---

[1] *Journal.*

[2] We notice this manner also in *The Woodcutters*, which was completed at the same period. For example : " There are three kinds of love : 1. æsthetic love ; 2. devoted love ; 3. active love," &c. (*Youth*). " There are three kinds of soldiers : 1. the docile and subordinate ; 2. the authoritative ; 3. the boasters—who themselves are subdivided into : (*a*) The docile who are cool and lethargic ; (*b*) those who are earnestly docile ; (*c*) docile soldiers who drink," &c. (*The Woodcutters*).

account of the forgotten sin ! An impassioned pan-
theism lends to certain pages a lyric beauty, whose
accents recall the tales of the Caucasus. For example,
this description of an evening in the spring :

"The calm splendour of the shining crescent ;
the gleaming fish-pond ; the ancient birch-trees,
whose long-tressed boughs were on one side
silvered by the moonlight, while on the other
they covered the path and the bushes with their
black shadows ; the cry of a quail beyond the
pond ; the barely perceptible sound of two
ancient trees which grazed one another ; the
humming of the mosquitoes ; the fall of an apple
on the dry leaves ; and the frogs leaping up to the
steps of the terrace, their backs gleaming greenish
under a ray of moonlight. . . . The moon is
mounting ; suspended in the limpid sky, she fills
all space with her light ; the splendour of the
moonlit water grows yet more brilliant, the shadows
grow blacker, the light more transparent. . . .
And to me, an obscure and earthy creature, already
soiled with every human passion, but endowed
with all the stupendous power of love, it seemed
at that moment that all nature, the moon, and I
myself were one and the same." [1]

But the present reality, potent and imperious,
spoke more loudly than the dreams of the past.
Youth remained unfinished ; and Captain Count
Tolstoy, behind the plating of his bastion, amid
the rumbling of the bombardment, or in the midst
of his company, observed the dying and the living,

[1] *Youth*, xxxii.

and recorded their miseries and his own, in his unforgettable narratives of *Sebastopol*.

These three narratives—*Sebastopol in December, 1854, Sebastopol in May, 1855, Sebastopol in August, 1855*—are generally confounded with one another; but in reality they present many points of difference. The second in particular, in point both of feeling and of art, is greatly superior to the others. The others are dominated by patriotism; the second is charged with implacable truth.

It is said that after reading the first narrative [1] the Tsarina wept, and the Tsar, moved by admiration, commanded that the story should be translated into French, and the author sent out of danger. We can readily believe it. Nothing in these pages but exalts warfare and the fatherland. Tolstoy had just arrived; his enthusiasm was intact; he was afloat on a tide of heroism. As yet he could see in the defenders of Sebastopol neither ambition nor vanity, nor any unworthy feeling. For him the war was a sublime epic; its heroes were " worthy of Greece." On the other hand, these notes exhibit no effort of the imagination, no attempt at objective representation. The writer strolls through the city; he sees with the utmost lucidity, but relates what he sees in a form which is wanting in freedom: "You see . . . you enter . . . you notice. . . ." This is first-class reporting; rich in admirable impressions.

Very different is the second scene: *Sebastopol in May, 1855*. In the opening lines we read:

[1] Sent to the review *Sovremennik* and immediately published.

"Here the self-love, the vanity of thousands of human beings is in conflict, or appeased in death. . . ."

And further on :

"And as there were many men, so also were there many forms of vanity. . . . Vanity, vanity, everywhere vanity, even at the door of the tomb ! It is the peculiar malady of our century. . . . Why do the Homers and Shakespeares speak of love, of glory, and of suffering, and why is the literature of our century nothing but the interminable history of snobs and egotists ? "

The narrative, which is no longer a simple narrative on the part of the author, but one which sets before us men and their passions, reveals that which is concealed by the mask of heroism. Tolstoy's clear, disillusioned gaze plumbs to the depths the hearts of his companions in arms ; in them, as in himself, he reads pride, fear, and the comedy of those who continue to play at life though rubbing shoulders with death. Fear especially is avowed, stripped of its veils, and shown in all its nakedness. These nervous crises,[1] this obsession of death, are analysed with a terrible sincerity that knows neither shame nor pity. It was at Sebastopol that Tolstoy

[1] Tolstoy refers to them again at a much later date, in his *Conversations* with his friend Teneromo. He tells him of a crisis of terror which assailed him one night when he was lying down in the "lodgement" dug out of the body of the rampart, under the protective plating. This *Episode of the Siege of Sebastopol* will be found in the volume entitled *The Revolutionaries.*

learned to eschew sentimentalism, "that vague, feminine, whimpering passion," as he came disdainfully to term it; and his genius for analysis, the instinct for which awoke, as we saw, in the later years of his boyhood, and which was at times to assume a quality almost morbid,[1] never attained to a more hypnotic and poignant intensity than in the narrative of the death of Praskhoukhin. Two whole pages are devoted to the description of all that passed in the mind of the unhappy man during the second following upon the fall of the shell, while the fuse was hissing towards explosion; and one page deals with all that passed before him after it exploded, when "he was killed on the spot by a fragment which struck him full in the chest."

As in the intervals of a drama we hear the occasional music of the orchestra, so these scenes of battle are interrupted by wide glimpses of nature; deep perspectives of light; the symphony of the day dawning upon the splendid landscape, in the midst of which thousands are agonising. Tolstoy the Christian, forgetting the patriotism of his first narrative, curses this impious war:

"And these men, Christians, who profess the

[1] Droujinine, a little later, wrote him a friendly letter in which he sought to put him on his guard against this danger: "You have a tendency to an excessive minuteness of analysis; it may become a serious fault. Sometimes you seem on the point of saying that so-and-so's calf indicated a desire to travel in the Indies. . . . You must restrain this tendency: but do not for the world suppress it." (Letter dated 1856 cited by P. Birukov.)

same great law of love and of sacrifice, do not, when they perceive what they have done, fall upon their knees repentant, before Him who in giving them life set within the heart of each, together with the fear of death, the love of the good and the beautiful. They do not embrace as brothers, with tears of joy and happiness ! "

As he was completing this novel—a work that has a quality of bitterness which, hitherto, none of his work had betrayed—Tolstoy was seized with doubt. Had he done wrong to speak ?

" A painful doubt assails me. Perhaps these things should not have been said. Perhaps what I am telling is one of those mischievous truths which, unconsciously hidden in the mind of each one of us, should not be expressed lest they become harmful, like the lees that we must not stir lest we spoil the wine. If so, when is the expression of evil to be avoided ? When is the expression of goodness to be imitated ? Who is the malefactor and who is the hero ? All are good and all are evil. . . ."

But he proudly regains his poise : " The protagonist of my novel, whom I love with all the strength of my soul, whom I try to present in all her beauty, who always was, is, and shall be beautiful, is Truth."

After reading these pages [1] Nekrasov, the editor of the review *Sovremennik*, wrote to Tolstoy:

" That is precisely what Russian society needs to-day : the truth, the truth, of which, since the

[1] Mutilated by the censor.

death of Gogol, so little has remained in Russian letters. . . . This truth which you bring to our art is something quite novel with us. I have only one fear : lest the times, and the cowardice of life, the deafness and dumbness of all that surrounds us, may make of you what it has made of most of us—lest it may kill the energy in you." [1]

Nothing of the kind was to be feared. The times, which waste the energies of ordinary men, only tempered those of Tolstóy. Yet for a moment the trials of his country and the capture of Sebastopol aroused a feeling of regret for· his perhaps too unfeeling frankness, together with a feeling of sorrowful affection.

In his third narrative — *Sebastopol in August, 1855*—while describing a group of officers playing cards and quarrelling, he interrupts himself to say :

"But let us drop the curtain quickly over this picture. To-morrow — perhaps to-day — each of these men will go cheerfully to meet his death. In the depths of the soul of each there smoulders the spark of nobility which will make him a hero."

Although this shame detracts in no wise from the forcefulness and realism of the narrative, the choice of characters shows plainly enough where lie the sympathies of the writer. The epic of Malakoff and its heroic fall is told as affecting two rare and touching figures : two brothers, of whom the elder, Kozeltoff, has some of the characteristics of Tolstoy. Who can forget the younger, the ensign

[1] September 2, 1855.

Volodya, timid and enthusiastic, with his feverish
monologues, his dreams, his tears ?—tears that rise
to his eyes for a mere nothing; tears of tenderness, tears of humiliation—his fear during the first
hours passed in the bastion (the poor boy is still
afraid of the dark, and covers his head with his
cloak when he goes to bed); the oppression caused
by the feeling of his own solitude and the indifference of others; then, when the hour arrives,
his joy in danger. He belongs to the group of
poetic figures of youth (of whom are Petia in *War
and Peace*, and the sub-lieutenant in *The Invasion*),
who, their hearts full of affection, make war with
laughter on their lips, and are broken suddenly,
uncomprehending, on the wheel of death. The
two brothers fall wounded, both on the same
day—the last day of the defence. The novel ends
with these lines, in which we hear the muttering
of a patriotic anger :

"The army was leaving the town; and each
soldier, as he looked upon deserted Sebastopol,
sighed, with an inexpressible bitterness in his
heart, and shook his fist in the direction of the
enemy."[1]

---

[1] In 1889, when writing a preface to *Memories of Sebastopol,
by an Officer of Artillery* (A. J. Erchoff), Tolstoy returned in
fancy to these scenes. Every heroic memory had disappeared.
He could no longer remember anything but the fear which
lasted for seven months—the double fear : the fear of death
and the fear of shame—and the horrible moral torture. All
the exploits of the siege reduced themselves, for him, to this :
he had been "flesh for cannon."

VI

ST. PETERSBURG

CHAPTER VI

ST. PETERSBURG

WHEN, once issued from this hell, where for a year he had touched the extreme of the passions, vanities, and sorrows of humanity, Tolstoy found himself, in November, 1855, amidst the men of letters of St. Petersburg, they inspired him with a feeling of disdain and disillusion. They seemed to him entirely mean, ill-natured, and untruthful. These men, who appeared in the distance to wear the halo of art—even Tourgenev, whom he had admired, and to whom he had but lately dedicated *The Woodcutters*—even he, seen close at hand, had bitterly disappointed him. A portrait of 1856 represents him in the midst of them: Tourgenev, Gontcharov, Ostrovsky, Grigorovitch, Droujinine. He strikes one, in the free-and-easy atmosphere of the others, by reason of his hard, ascetic air, his bony head, his lined cheeks, his rigidly folded arms. Standing upright, in uniform, behind these men of letters, he has the appearance, as Suarès has wittily said, "rather of mounting guard over these gentry than of making one of their company;

61

as though he were ready to march them back to gaol." [1]

Yet they all gathered about their young colleague, who came to them with the twofold glory of the writer and the hero of Sebastopol. Tourgenev, who had "wept and shouted ' Hurrah ! '" while reading the pages of *Sebastopol*, held out a brotherly hand. But the two men could not understand one another. Although both saw the world with the same clear vision, they mingled with that vision the hues of their inimical minds ; the one, ironic, resonant, amorous, disillusioned, a devotee of beauty; the other proud, violent tormented with moral ideas, pregnant with a hidden God.

What Tolstoy could never forgive in these literary men was that they believed themselves an elect, superior caste ; the crown of humanity. Into his antipathy for them there entered a good deal of the pride of the great noble and the officer who condescendingly mingles with liberal and middle-class scribblers. [2] It was also a characteristic of his—he himself knew it—to " oppose instinctively all trains of reasoning, all conclusions, which were generally admitted." [3] A distrust of mankind, a latent con-

---

[1] Suarès : *Tolstoï*, edition of the *Union pour l'Action morale*, 1899 (reprinted, in the *Cahiers de la Quinzaine*, under the title *Tolstoï vivant*).

[2] Tourgenev complained, in a conversation, of "this stupid nobleman's pride, his bragging Junkerdom."

[3] "A trait of my character, it may be good or ill, but it is one which was always peculiar to me, is that in spite of myself I always used to resist external epidemic influences . . . . I had a hatred of the general tendency." (Letter to P. Birukov.)

tempt for human reason, made him always on the alert to discover deception in himself or others.

"He never believed in the sincerity of any one. All moral exhilaration seemed false to him; and he had a way of fixing, with that extraordinarily piercing gaze of his, the man whom he suspected was not telling the truth."[1] "How he used to listen! How he used to gaze at those who spoke to him, from the very depths of his grey eyes, deeply sunken in their orbits! With what irony his lips were pressed together!"[2]

"Tourgenev used to say that he had never experienced anything more painful than this piercing gaze, which, together with two or three words of envenomed observation, was capable of infuriating anybody."[3]

At their first meetings violent scenes occurred between Tolstoy and Tourgenev. When at a distance they cooled down and tried to do one another justice. But as time went on Tolstoy's dislike of his literary surroundings grew deeper. He could not forgive these artists for the combination of their depraved life and their moral pretensions.

"I acquired the conviction that nearly all were immoral men, unsound, without character, greatly inferior to those I had met in my Bohemian military life. And they were sure of themselves and self-content, as men might be who were absolutely sound. They disgusted me."[4]

[1] Tourgenev.   [2] Grigorovitch.
[3] Eugène Gardine : *Souvenirs sur Tourgeniev*, 1883. See *Vie et Œuvre de Tolstoï*, by Birukov.   [4] *Confessions.*

He parted from them. But he did not at once lose their interested faith in art.[1] His pride was flattered thereby. It was a faith which was richly rewarded ; it brought him "women, money, fame."

"Of this religion I was one of the pontiffs ; an agreeable and highly profitable situation."

The better to consecrate himself to this religion, he sent in his resignation from the army (November, 1856).

But a man of his temper could not close his eyes for long. He believed, he was eager to believe, in progress. It seemed to him "that this word signified something." A journey abroad, which lasted from the end of January to the end of July of 1857, during which period he visited France, Switzerland, and Germany, resulted in the destruction of this faith. In Paris, on the 6th of April, 1857, the spectacle of a public execution "showed him the emptiness of the superstition of progress."

"When I saw the head part from the body and fall into the basket I understood in every recess of my being that no theory as to the reason of the present order of things could justify such an act. Even though all the men in the world, supported by this or that theory, were to find it necessary, I myself should know that it was wrong ;

---

[1] "There was no difference between us and an asylum full of lunatics. Even at the time I vaguely suspected as much ; but as all madmen do, I regarded them as all mad excepting myself."—*Confessions*.

for it is not what men say or do that decides what is good or bad, but my own heart." [1]

In the month of July the sight of a little perambulating singer at Lucerne, to whom the wealthy English visitors at the Schweizerhof were refusing alms, made him express in the *Diary of Prince D. Nekhludov* his contempt for all the illusions dear to Liberals, and for those "who trace imaginary lines upon the sea of good and evil."

"For them civilisation is good; barbarism is bad; liberty is good; slavery is bad. And this imaginary knowledge destroys the instinctive, primordial cravings, which are the best. Who will define them for me—liberty, despotism, civilisation, barbarism? Where does not good co-exist with evil? There is within us only one infallible guide: the universal Spirit which whispers to us to draw closer to one another."

On his return to Russia and Yasnaya he once more busied himself about the peasants. Not that he had any illusions left concerning them. He writes:

"The apologists of the people and its good sense speak to no purpose; the crowd is perhaps the union of worthy folk; but if so they unite only on their bestial and contemptible side, a side which expresses nothing but the weakness and cruelty of human nature." [2]

Thus he does not address himself to the crowd, but to the individual conscience of each man, each child of the people. For there light is to be found.

[1] *Confessions.*   [2] *Diary of Prince D. Nekhludov.*

He founded schools, without precisely knowing what he would teach. In order to learn, he undertook another journey abroad, which lasted from the 3rd of July, 1860, to the 23rd of April, 1861.[1]

He studied the various pedagogic systems of the time. Need we say that he rejected one and all? Two visits to Marseilles taught him that the true education of the people is effected outside the schools (which he considered absurd), by means of the journals, the museums, the libraries, the street, and everyday life, which he termed "the spontaneous school." The spontaneous school, in opposition to the obligatory school, which he considered silly and harmful; this was what he wished and attempted to institute upon his return to Yasnaya Polyana.[2] Liberty was his principle. He would not admit that an elect class, "the privileged Liberal circle," should impose its knowledge and its errors upon "the people, to whom it is a stranger." It had no right to do so. This method of forced education had never succeeded in producing, at the University, "the men of whom humanity has need; but men of whom a depraved society has need; officials, official professors, official literary men, or men torn aimlessly from their old surroundings, whose youth has been spoiled and wasted, and who can find no plan in

[1] At Dresden, during his travels he made the acquaintance of Auerbach, who had been the first to inspire him with the idea of educating the people; at Kissingen he met Froebel, in London Herzen, and in Brussels Proudhon, who seems to have made a great impression upon him.

[2] Especially in 1861–62.

life : irritable, puny Liberals."[1] Go to the people
to learn what they want ! If they do not value
"the art of reading and writing which the intellectuals force upon them," they have their
reasons for that ; they have other spiritual needs,
more pressing and more legitimate. Try to understand those needs, and help them to satisfy them !

These theories, those of a revolutionary Conservative, as Tolstoy always was, he attempted to put
into practice at Yasnaya, where he was rather the
fellow-disciple than the master of his pupils.[2] At
the same time, he endeavoured to introduce a
new human spirit into agricultural exploitation.
Appointed in 1861 territorial arbitrator for the
district of Krapiona, he was the people's cham-
pion against the abuses of power on the part
of the landowners and the State.

We must not suppose that this social activity
satisfied him, or entirely filled his life. He continued
to be the prey of contending passions. Although he
had suffered from the world, he always loved it and
felt the need of it. Pleasure resumed him at
intervals, or else the love of action. He would risk
his life in hunting the bear. He played for heavy
stakes. He would even fall under the influence of
the literary circles of St. Petersburg, for which he
felt such contempt. After these aberrations came
crises of disgust. Such of his writings as belong to

[1] *Education and Culture.* See *Vie et Œuvre*, by Birukov,
vol. ii.

[2] Tolstoy explained these principles in the review *Yasnaya
Polyana*, 1862.

this period bear unfortunate traces of this artistic
and moral uncertainty. *The Two Hussars* (1856) has
a quality of pretentiousness and elegance, a snobbish
worldly flavour, which shocks one as coming from
Tolstoy. *Albert*, written at Dijon in 1857, is weak
and eccentric, with no trace of the writer's habitual
depth or precision. The *Diary of a Sportsman*
(1856), a more striking though hasty piece of work,
seems to betray the disillusionment which Tolstoy
inspired in himself. Prince Nekhludov, his *Doppel-
ganger*, his double, kills himself in a gaming-house.

"He had everything : wealth, a name, intellect,
and high ambitions ; he had committed no crime ;
but he had done still worse : he had killed his
courage, his youth ; he was lost, without even the
excuse of a violent passion ; merely from a lack
of will."

The approach of death itself does not alter him :

"The same strange inconsequence, the same
hesitation, the same frivolity of thought. . . ."

Death ! . . . At this period it began to haunt
his mind. *Three Deaths* (1858-59) already fore-
shadowed the gloomy analysis of *The Death of Ivan
Ilyitch ;* the solitude of the dying man, his hatred of
the living, his desperate query — "Why ?" The
triptych of the three deaths—that of the wealthy
woman, that of the old consumptive postilion, and
that of the slaughtered dog—is not without majesty ;
the portraits are well drawn, the images are striking,
although the whole work, which has been too highly
praised, is somewhat loosely constructed, while the
death of the dog lacks the poetic precision to be

found in the writer's beautiful landscapes. Taking it as a whole, we hardly know how far it is intended as a work of art for the sake of art, or whether it has a moral intention.

Tolstoy himself did not know. On the 4th of February, 1858, when he read his essay of admittance before the *Muscovite Society of Amateurs of Russian Literature*, he chose for his subject the defence of art for art's sake.[1] It was the president of the Society, Khomiakov, who, after saluting in Tolstoy "the representative of purely artistic literature," took up the defence of social and moral art.[2]

A year later the death of his dearly-loved brother, Nikolas, who succumbed to phthisis[3] at Hyères, on the 19th of September, 1860, completely overcame

---

[1] Lecture on *The Superiority of the Artistic Element in Literature over all its Contemporary Tendencies.*

He cited against Tolstoy his own examples, including the old postilion in *The Three Deaths.*

[3] We may remark that another brother, Dmitri, had already died of the same disease in 1856. Tolstoy himself believed that he was attacked by it in 1856, in 1862, and in 1871. He was, as he writes (the 28th of October, 1852), "of a strong constitution, but feeble in health." He constantly suffered from chills, sore throats, toothache, inflamed eyes, and rheumatism. In the Caucasus, in 1852, he had "two days in the week at least to keep his room." Illness stopped him for several months in 1854, on the road from Silistria to Sebastopol. In 1856, at Yasnaya, he was seriously ill with an affection of the lungs. In 1862 the fear of phthisis induced him to undergo a *Koumiss* cure at Samara, where he lived with the Bachkirs, and after 1870 he returned thither almost yearly. His correspondence with Fet is full of preoccupations

Tolstoy ; shook him to the point of "crushing his faith in goodness, in everything," and made him deny even his art :

"Truth is horrible. . . . Doubless, so long as the desire to know and to speak the truth exists men will try to know and to speak it. This is the only remnant left me of my moral concepts. It is the only thing I shall do ; but not in the form of art, your art. Art is a lie, and I can no longer love a beautiful lie." [1]

Less than six months later, however, he returned to the "beautiful lie" with *Polikushka*,[2] which of all his works is perhaps most devoid of moral intention, if we except the latent malediction upon money and its powers for evil ; a work written purely for art's sake ; a masterpiece, moreover, whose only flaws are a possibly excessive wealth of observation, an abundance of material which would have sufficed for a great novel, and the contrast, which is

concerning his health. This physical condition enables one the better to understand his obsession by the thought of death. In later years he spoke of this illness as of his best friend :

"When one is ill one seems to descend a very gentle slope, which at a certain point is barred by a curtain, a light curtain of some filmy stuff ; on the hither side is life, beyond is death. How far superior is the state of illness, in moral value, to that of health ! Do not speak to me of those people who have never been ill ! They are terrible, the women especially so ! A woman who has never known illness is an absolute wild beast !" (Conversations with M. Paul Boyer, *Le Temps*, 27th of August, 1901.)

[1] Letter to Fet, October 17, 1860 (*Further Letters* : in the French version, *Correspondance inédite*, pp. 27—30).

[2] Written in Brussels, 1861.

too severe, a little too cruel, between the humorous opening and the atrocious climax.[1]

---

[1] Another novel written at this period is a simple narrative of a journey—*The Snowstorm*—which evokes personal memories, and is full of the beauty of poetic and quasi-musical impressions. Tolstoy used almost the same background later, in his *Master and Servant* (1895).

VII

"FAMILY
HAPPINESS"

CHAPTER VII

"FAMILY HAPPINESS"

FROM this period of transition, during which the genius of the man was feeling its way blindly, doubtful of itself and apparently exhausted, "devoid of strong passion, without a directing will," like Nekhludov in the *Diary of a Sportsman*—from this period issued a work unique in its tenderness and charm : *Family Happiness* (1859). This was the miracle of love.

For many years Tolstoy had been on friendly terms with the Bers family. He had fallen in love with the mother and the three daughters in succession.[1] His final choice fell upon the second, but he dared not confess it. Sophie Andreyevna Bers was still a child ; she was seventeen years old, while Tolstoy was over thirty ; he regarded himself as an old man, who had not the right to associate his soiled and vitiated life with that of an innocent

---

[1] When a child he had, in a fit of jealousy, pushed from a balcony the little girl—then aged nine—who afterwards became Madame Bers, with the result that she was lame for several years.

LIBRARY
OF
MOUNT ST. MARY'S
COLLEGE
EMMITSBURG, MARYLAND

young girl. He held out for three years.[1] Afterwards, in *Anna Karenin*, he related how his declaration to Sophie Bers was effected, and how she replied to it : both of them tracing with one finger, under a table, the initials of words they dared not say.

Like Levine in *Anna Karenin*, he was so cruelly honest as to place his intimate journal in the hands of his betrothed, in order that she should be unaware of none of his past transgressions ; and Sophie, like Kitty in *Anna Karenin*, was bitterly hurt by its perusal. They were married on the 23rd of September, 1862.

In the artist's imagination this marriage was consummated three years earlier, when *Family Happiness* was written.[2] For these years he had been living in the future ; through the ineffable days of love that does not as yet know itself : through the delirious days of love that has attained self-knowledge, and the hour in which the divine, anticipated words are whispered ; when the tears arise "of a happiness which departs for ever and will never return again" ; and the triumphant reality of

[1] See, in *Family Happiness*, the declaration of Sergius : "Suppose there were a Mr. A, an elderly man who had lived his life, and a lady B, young and happy, who as yet knew neither men nor life. As the result of various domestic happenings, he came to love her as a daughter, and was not aware that he could love her in another way . . . " &c.

[2] Perhaps this novel contained the memories also of a romantic love affair which commenced in 1856, in Moscow, the second party to which was a young girl very different to himself, very worldly and frivolous, from whom he finally parted, although they were sincerely attached to one another.

the early days of marriage ; the egoism of lovers, "the incessant, causeless joy," then the approaching weariness, the vague discontent, the boredom of a monotonous life, the two souls which softly disengage themselves and grow further and further away from one another ; the dangerous attraction of the world for the young wife—flirtations, jealousies, fatal mis-understandings ;—love dissimulated, love lost ; and at length the sad and tender autumn of the heart ; the face of love which reappears, paler, older, but more touching by reason of tears and the marks of time ; the memory of troubles, the regret for the ill things done and the years that are lost ; the calm of the evening; the august passage from love to friend-ship, and the romance of the passion of maternity. . . . All that was to come, all this Tolstoy had dreamed of, tasted in advance ; and in order to live through those days more vividly he lived in the well-beloved. For the first time—perhaps the only time in all his writings—the story passes in the heart of a woman, and is told by her ; and with what exquisite delicacy, what spiritual beauty !— the beauty of a soul withdrawn behind a veil of the truest modesty. For once the analysis of the writer is deprived of its cruder lights ; there is no feverish struggle to present the naked truth. The secrets of the inward life are divined rather than spoken. The art and the heart of the artist are both touched and softened ; there is a harmonious balance of thought and form. *Family Happiness* has the per-fection of a work of Racine.

Marriage, whose sweet and bitter Tolstoy presented with so limpid a profundity, was to be his salvation. He was tired, unwell, disgusted with himself and his efforts. The brilliant success which had crowned his earlier works had given way to the absolute silence of the critics and the indifference of the public.[1] He pretended, haughtily, to be not ill-pleased.

"My reputation has greatly diminished in popularity; a fact which was saddening me. Now I am content; I know that I have to say something, and that I have the power to speak it with no feeble voice. As for the public, let it think what it will!"[2]

But he was boasting: he himself was not sure of his art. Certainly he was the master of his literary instrument; but he did not know what to do with it, as he said in respect of *Polikuskha*: "it was a matter of chattering about the first subject that came to hand, by a man who knows how to hold his pen."[3] His social work was abortive. In 1862 he resigned his appointment as territorial arbitrator. The same year the police made a search at Yasnaya Polyana, turned everything topsy-turvy, and closed the school. Tolstoy was absent at the time, suffering from overwork; fearing that he was attacked by phthisis.

"The squabbles of arbitration had become so painful to me, the work of the school so vague, and the doubts which arose from the desire of teaching others while hiding my own ignorance

---

[1] From 1857 to 1861.
[2] *Journal*, October, 1857.
[3] Letter to Fet, 1863 (*Vie et Œuvre*).

of what had to be taught, were so disheartening that I fell ill. Perhaps I should then have fallen into the state of despair to which I was to succumb fifteen years later, had there not remained to me an unknown aspect of life which promised salvation—the life of the family." [1]

[1] *Confessions.*

VIII

MARRIAGE

CHAPTER VIII

MARRIAGE

AT first he rejoiced in the new life, with the passion which he brought to everything.[1] The personal influence of Countess Tolstoy was a godsend to his art. Greatly gifted[2] in a literary sense, she was, as she says, "a true author's wife," so keenly did she take her husband's work to heart. She worked with him—worked to his dictation; re-copied his rough drafts.[3] She sought to protect him from his religious dæmon, that formidable genie which was already, at moments, whispering words that meant the death of art. She tried to shut the door upon all social Utopias.[4] She requickened her husband's creative genius. She did more : she brought as an offering to that genius the wealth of a fresh feminine temperament. With the exception of the charming

[1] "Domestic happiness completely absorbs me" (January 5, 1863). "I am so happy ! so happy ! I love her so !" (February 8, 1863). See *Vie et Œuvre*.

[2] She had written several novels.

[3] It is said that she copied *War and Peace* seven times.

[4] Directly after his marriage Tolstoy suspended his work of teaching, his review, and his school.

silhouettes in *Childhood* and *Boyhood*, there are few women in the earlier works of Tolstoy, or they remain of secondary importance. Woman appears in *Family Happiness*, written under the influence of his love for Sophie Bers. In the works which follow there are numerous types of young girls and women, full of intensest life, and even superior to the male types. One likes to think not only that Countess Tolstoy served her husband as the model for Natasha in *War and Peace*[1] and for Kitty in *Anna Karenin*,[2] but that she was enabled, by means of her confidences and her own vision, to become his discreet and valuable collaborator. Certain pages of *Anna Karenin* in particular seem to me to reveal a woman's touch.

Thanks to the advantages of this union, Tolstoy enjoyed for a space of twelve or fourteen years a peace and security which had been long unknown to him.[3] He was able, sheltered by love, to dream

[1] Her sister Tatiana, intelligent and artistic, whose wit and musical talent were greatly admired by Tolstoy, also served him as a model. Tolstoy used to say, "I took Tania [Tatiana]; I beat her up with Sonia [Sophie Bers, Countess Tolstoy], and out came Natasha" (cited by P. Birukov).

[2] The installation of Dolly in the tumble-down country house; Dolly and the children; a number of details of dress and toilet; without speaking of certain secrets of the feminine mind, which even the intuition of a man of genius might perhaps have failed to penetrate, if a woman had not betrayed them to him.

[3] Here is a characteristic instance of Tolstoy's enslavement by his creative genius: his *Journal* is interrupted for thirteen years, from November 1, 1865, when the composition of *War and Peace* was in full swing. The egoism of the artist has

and to realise at leisure the masterpieces of his
brain, the colossal monuments which dominate the
fiction of the nineteenth century—*War and Peace*
(1864–69) and *Anna Karenin* (1873–77).

War and Peace is the vastest epic of our times—
a modern *Iliad*. A world of faces and of passions
moves within it. Over this human ocean of in-
numerable waves broods a sovereign mind, which
serenely raises or stills the tempest.

More than once in the past, while contemplating
this work, I was reminded of Homer and of Goethe,
in spite of the vastly different spirit and period of
the work. Since then I have discovered that at
the period of writing these books Tolstoy was as
a matter of fact nourishing his mind upon Homer
and Goethe.[1] Moreover, in the notes, dated 1865,

silenced the monologue of the conscience.—This period of
creation was also a period of robust physical life. Tolstoy
was "mad on hunting." "Hunting, I forget everything. . . ."
(Letter of 1864.) In September, 1864, during a hunt on horse
back, he broke his arm, and it was during his convalescence
that the first portions of *War and Peace* were dictated.—" On
recovering consciousness after fainting, I said to myself : ' I
am an artist.' And I am, but a lonely artist." (Letter to Fet,
January 29, 1865.) All the letters written at this time to Fet
are full of an exulting joy of creation. " I regard all that I
have hitherto published," he says, " as merely a trial of my
pen." (*Ibid.*)

[1] Before this date Tolstoy had noted, among the books
which influenced him between the ages of twenty and thirty-
five :

" Goethe : *Hermann and Dorothea*—Very great influence."

" Homer : *Iliad and Odyssey* (in Russian)—Very great
influence."

in which he classifies the various departments of letters, he mentions, as belonging to the same family, " Odyssey, Iliad, 1805." [1] The natural development of his mind led him from the romance of individual destinies to the romance of armies and peoples, those vast human hordes in which the wills of millions of beings are dissolved. His tragic experiences at the siege of Sebastopol helped him to comprehend the soul of the Russian nation and its daily life. According to his first intentions, the gigantic *War and Peace* was to be merely the central panel of a series of epic frescoes, in which the poem of Russia should be developed from Peter the Great to the Decembrists.[2]

And in June, 1863, he notes in his diary :

" I am reading Goethe, and many ideas are coming to life within me."

In the spring of 1863 Tolstoy was re-reading Goethe, and wrote of *Faust* as " the poetry of the world of thought ; the poetry which expresses that which can be expressed by no other art."

Later he sacrificed Goethe, as he did Shakespeare, to his God. But he remained faithful in his admiration of Homer. In August, 1857, he was reading, with equal zest, the *Iliad* and the Bible. In one of his latest works, the pamphlet attacking Shakespeare (1903), it is Homer that he opposes to Shakespeare as an example of sincerity, balance, and true art.

[1] The two first parts of *War and Peace* appeared in 1865–66 under the title *The Year 1805.*

[2] Tolstoy commenced this work in 1863 by *The Decembrists,* of which he wrote three fragments. But he saw that the foundations of his plan were not sufficiently assured, and going further back, to the period of the Napoleonic Wars, he wrote *War and Peace.* Publication was commenced in the *Rousski Viestnik* of January, 1865 ; the sixth volume was completed in the autumn of 1869. Then Tolstoy ascended the

To be truly sensible of the power of this work,
we must take into account its hidden unity. Too
many readers, unable to see it in perspective, perceive in it nothing but thousands of details, whose
profusion amazes and distracts them. They are lost
in this forest of life. The reader must stand aloof,
upon a height; he must attain the view of the un-
obstructed horizon, the vast circle of forest and
meadow; then he will catch the Homeric spirit
of the work, the calm of eternal laws, the awful
rhythm of the breathing of Destiny, the sense of

stream of history; and he conceived the plan of an epic
romance dealing with Peter the Great; then of another,
Mirovitch, dealing with the rule of the Empresses of the
eighteenth century and their favourites. He worked at it
from 1870 to 1873, surrounded with documents, and writing
the first drafts of various portions; but his realistic scruples
made him renounce the project: he was conscious that he
could never succeed in resuscitating the spirit of those
distant periods in a sufficiently truthful fashion. Later, in
January, 1876, he conceived the idea of another romance of
the period of Nikolas I.; then he eagerly returned to the
Decembrists, collecting the evidence of survivors and visiting
the scenes of the action. In 1878 he wrote to his aunt, Countess
A. A. Tolstoy: " This work is so important to me! You
cannot imagine how much it means to me; it is as much to
me as your faith is to you. I would say even more." (*Correspondence.*)   But in proportion as he plumbed the subject
he grew away from it; his heart was in it no longer. As
early as April, 1879, he wrote to Fet: " *The Decembrists?* If I
were thinking of it, if I were to write it, I should flatter
myself with the hope that the very atmosphere of my mind
would be insupportable to those who fire upon men for the
good of humanity." (*Ibid.*)   At this period of his life the
religious crisis had set in; he was about to burn his ancient
idols.

the whole of which every detail makes a part; and
the genius of the artist, supreme over the whole,
like the God of Genesis who broods upon the face
of the waters.

In the beginning, the calm of the ocean. Peace, and
the life of Russia before the war. The first hundred
pages reflect, with an impassive precision, a detached
irony, the yawning emptiness of worldly minds.
Only towards the hundredth page do we hear the
cry of one of these living dead—the worst among
them, Prince Basil :

" We commit sins ; we deceive one another; and
why do we do it all ? My friend, I am more than
sixty years old. . . . All ends in death. . . . Death—
what horror ! "

Among these idle, insipid, untruthful souls,
capable of every aberration, of every crime, certain saner natures are prominent : genuine natures
by their clumsy candour, like Pierre Besoukhov ; by
their deeply rooted independence, their Old Russian
peculiarities, like Marie Dmitrievna ; by the freshness of their youth, like the little Rostoffs : natures
full of goodness and resignation, like the Princess
Marie ; and those who, like Prince Andrei, are not
good, but proud, and are tormented by an unhealthy
existence.

Now comes the first muttering of the waves. The
Russian army is in Austria. Fatality is supreme :
nowhere more visibly imperious than in the loosing
of elementary forces—in the war. The true leaders
are those who do not seek to lead or direct, but,
like Kutuzov or Bagration, to " allow it to be

believed that their personal intentions are in perfect agreement with what is really the simple result of the force of circumstances, the will of subordinates, and the caprices of chance." The advantage of surrendering to the hand of Destiny! The happiness of simple action, a sane and normal state. . . . The troubled spirits regain their poise. Prince Andrei breathes, begins to live. . . . And while in the far distance, remote from the life-giving breath of the holy tempest, Pierre and the Princess Marie are threatened by the contagion of their world and the deception of love, Andrei, wounded at Austerlitz, has suddenly, amid the intoxication of action brutally interrupted, the revelation of the serene immensity of the universe. Lying on his back, " he sees nothing now, except, very far above him, a sky infinitely deep, wherein light, greyish clouds go softly wandering."

"What peacefulness! How calm!" he was saying to himself; "it was not like this when I was running by and shouting. . . . How was it I did not notice it before, this illimitable depth? How happy I am to have found it at last! Yes, all is emptiness, all is deception, except this. And God be praised for this calm!. . ."

But life resumes him, and again the wave falls. Left once more to themselves, in the demoralising atmosphere of cities, the restless, discouraged souls wander blindly in the darkness. Sometimes through the poisoned atmosphere of the world sweep the intoxicating, maddening odours of nature, love, and springtime; the blind forces, which draw together Prince Andrei and the charming Natasha, to throw her, a moment later, into the arms of the first seducer to hand. So much poetry, so much tenderness, so much purity of heart, tarnished by the world ! And always "the wide sky which broods above the outrage and abjectness of the earth." But man does not see it. Even Andrei has forgotten the light of Austerlitz. For him the sky is now only "a dark, heavy vault" which covers the face of emptiness.

It is time for the hurricane of war to burst once more upon these vitiated minds. The fatherland, Russia, is invaded. Then comes the day of Borodino, with its solemn majesty. Enmities are effaced. Dologhov embraces his enemy Pierre. Andrei, wounded, weeps for pity and compassion over the misery of the man whom he most hated, Anatol Kuraguin, his neighbour in the ambulance. The unity of hearts is accomplished ; unity in passionate sacrifice to the country and submission to the divine laws.

"To accept the frightful necessity of war, seriously and austerely. . . . To human liberty, war is the most painful act of submission to the divine laws. Simplicity of heart consists in submission to the will of God."

The soul of the Russian people and its submission to Destiny are incarnated in the person of the commander-in-chief, Kutuzov. "This old man, who has no passions left, but only experience, the result of the passions, and in whom intelligence, which is intended to group together facts and to draw from them conclusions, is replaced by a philosophical contemplation of events, devises nothing and undertakes nothing ; but he listens to and remembers everything ; he knows how to profit by it at the right moment ; he will hinder nothing that is of use, he will permit nothing harmful. He sees on the faces of his troops that inexpressible force which is known as the will to conquer ; it is latent victory. He admits something more powerful than his own will : the inevitable march of the facts which pass before his eyes ; he sees them, he follows them, and he is able mentally to stand aloof."

In short, he has the heart of a Russian. This fatalism of the Russian people, calmly heroic, is personified also in the poor moujik, Platon Kara- tayev, simple, pious, and resigned, with his kindly patient smile in suffering and in death. Through suffering and experience, above the ruins of their country, after the horrors of its agony, Pierre and Andrei, the two heroes of the book, attain, through love and faith, to the moral deliverance and the mystic joy by which they behold God living.

Tolstoy does not stop here. The epilogue, of which the action passes in 1820, deals with the transition from one age to another : from one Napoleonic era to the era of the Decembrists. It produces an impression of continuity, and of the resumption of life. Instead of commencing and ending in the midst of a crisis, Tolstoy finishes, as he began, at the moment when a great wave has

spent itself, while that following it is gathering
itself together. Already we obtain a glimpse of the
heroes to be, of the conflicts which will ensue
between them, and of the dead who are born
again in the living.[1]

I have tried to indicate the broad lines of the
romance ; for few readers take the trouble to look
for them. But what words are adequate to describe
the extraordinary vitality of these hundreds of
heroes, all distinct individuals, all drawn with
unforgettable mastery : soldiers, peasants, great

---

[1] Pierre Besoukhov, who has married Natasha, will become a Decembrist. He has founded a secret society to
watch over the general good, a sort of *Tugelbund*. Natasha
associates herself with his plans with the utmost enthusiasm.
Denissov cannot conceive of a pacific revolution ; but is
quite ready for an armed revolt. Nikolas Rostoff has retained
his blind soldier's loyalty. He who said before Austerlitz,
" We have only one thing to do : to fight and never to think,"
is angry with Pierre, and exclaims : " My oath before all !
If I were ordered to march against you with my squadron
I should march and I should strike home." His wife,
Princess Marie, agrees with him. Prince Andrei's son, little
Nikolas Bolkonsky, fifteen years old, delicate, sickly, yet
charming, with wide eyes and golden hair, listens feverishly
to the discussion ; all his love is Pierre's and Natasha's ; he
does not care greatly for Nikolas and Marie ; he worships
his father, whom he has never seen ; he dreams of growing
like him, of being grown up, of doing something wonderful,
he knows not what. " Whatever they tell me, I will do it.
. . . Yes, I shall do it. *He* would have been pleased with
me."—And the book ends with the dream of a child, who
sees himself in the guise of one of Plutarch's heroes, with his
uncle Pierre by his side, preceded by Glory, and followed by
an army.—If the *Decembrists* had been written then little
Bolkonsky would doubtless have been one of its heroes.

nobles, Russians, Austrians, Frenchmen ! Not a
line savours of improvisation. For this gallery
of portraits, unexampled in European literature,
Tolstoy made sketches without number : " combined," as he says, " millions of projects " ; buried
himself in libraries ; laid under contribution his
family archives,[1] his previous notes, his personal
memories. This meticulous preparation ensured
the solidity of the work, but did not damp his
spontaneity. Tolstoy worked with enthusiasm,
with an eagerness and a delight which communicate
themselves to the reader. Above all, the great
charm of *War and Peace* resides in its spirit of
youth. No other work of Tolstoy's presents in
such abundance the soul of childhood and of
youth ; and each youthful spirit is a strain of music,
pure as a spring, full of a touching and penetrating grace, like a melody of Mozart's. Of such are
the young Nikolas Rostoff, Sonia, and poor little
Petia.

Most exquisite of all is Natasha. Dear little
girl !—fantastic, full of laughter, her heart full of
affection, we see her grow up before us, we follow
her through life, with the tenderness one would feel
for a sister—who that has read of her does not feel
that he has known her ? . . . That wonderful night
of spring, when Natasha, at her window, flooded

[1] I have remarked that the two families Rostoff and
Bolkonsky, in *War and Peace*, recall the families of Tolstoy's
father and mother by many characteristics. Again, in the
novels of the Caucasus and Sebastopol there are many of the
types of soldiers, officers and men, which appear in *War and
Peace*.

with the moonlight, dreams and speaks wildly, above the window of the listening Andrei ... the emotions of the first ball, the expectation of love, the burgeoning of riotous dreams and desires, the sleigh-ride, the night in the snow-bound forest, full of fantastic lights ; Nature, and the embrace of her vague tenderness: the evening at the Opera, the unfamiliar world of art, in which reason grows confused ; the folly of the heart, and the folly of the body yearning for love ; the misery that floods the soul; the divine pity which watches over the dying lover. ... One cannot evoke these pitiful memories without emotion ; such emotion as one would feel in speaking of a dear and beloved woman. How such a creation shows the weakness of the female types in almost the whole of contemporary drama and fiction ! Life itself has been captured ; life so fluid, so supple, that we seem to see it throbbing and changing from one line to another.

Princess Marie, the ugly woman, whose goodness makes her beautiful, is no less perfect a portrait ; but how the timid, awkward girl would have blushed, how those who resemble her must blush, at finding unveiled all the secrets of a heart which hides itself so fearfully from every glance !

In general the portraits of women are, as I have said, very much finer than the male characters ; in especial than those of the two heroes to whom Tolstoy has given his own ideas : the weak, pliable nature of Pierre Besoukhov, and the hard, eager nature of Prince Andrie Bolkonsky. These are characters which lack a centre of gravity ; they oscillate perpetually, rather than evolve; they run from one extreme to the other, yet never advance. One may, of course, reply that in this they are thoroughly Russian. I find, however, that Russians have criticised them in similar terms. Tourgenev doubtless had them in mind when he complained that Tolstoy's psychology was a stationary matter. "No real development. Eternal hesitations : oscillations of feeling." [1] Tolstoy himself admitted that he had at times rather sacrificed the individual character to the historical design. [2]

It is true, in fact, that the glory of *War and Peace* resides in the resurrection of a complete historical period, with its national migrations, its warfare of peoples. Its true heroes are these peoples; and behind them, as behind the heroes of Homer, the gods who lead them ; the forces, invisible, " infinitely small, which direct the masses," the breath of the Infinite. These gigantic conflicts, in which a hidden destiny hurls the blind nations together, have a mythical grandeur. Our thoughts go beyond the *Iliad :* we are reminded of the Hindu epics.

[1] Letter of February 2, 1868, cited by Birukov.
[2] Notably, he said, that of Prince Andrei in the first part.

IX

"ANNA KARENIN"

CHAPTER IX

"ANNA KARENIN"

Anna Karenin, with *War and Peace,*[1] marks the climax of this period of maturity. *Anna Karenin* is the more perfect work; the work of a mind more certain of its artistic creation, richer too in experience; a mind for which the world of the heart holds no more secrets. But it lacks the fire of youth, the freshness of enthusiasm, the mighty pinions of *War and Peace.* Already Tolstoy has lost something of the joy of creation.

[1] It is regrettable that the beauty of the poetical conception of the work is often tarnished by the philosophical chatter with which Tolstoy has loaded his work, especially in the later portions. He is determined to make an exposition of his theory of the fatality of history. The pity is that he returns to the point incessantly, and obstinately repeats himself. Flaubert, who "gave vent to cries of admiration" while reading the first two volumes, which he declared "sublime" and "full of Shakespearean things," threw the third volume aside in boredom : "He goes off horribly. He repeats himself, and he philosophises. We see the aristocrat, the author, and the Russian, while hitherto we have seen nothing but Nature and Humanity." (Letter to Tourgenev, January, 1880.)

The temporary peace of the first months of marriage has flown. Into the enchanted circle of love and art which Countess Tolstoy had drawn about him moral scruples begin to intrude.

Even in the early chapters of *War and Peace*, written one year after marriage, the confidences of Prince Andrei to Pierre upon the subject of marriage denote the disenchantment of the man who sees in the beloved woman the stranger, the innocent enemy, the involuntary obstacle to his moral development. Some letters of 1865 announce the coming return of religious troubles. As yet they are only passing threats, blotting out the joy of life. But during the months of 1869, when Tolstoy was finishing *War and Peace*, there fell a more serious blow.

He had left his home for a few days to visit a distant estate. One night he was lying in bed; it had just struck two:

" I was dreadfully tired; I was sleepy, and felt comfortable enough. All of a sudden I was seized by such anguish, such terror as I had never felt in all my life. I will tell you about it in detail; it was truly frightful. I leapt from the bed and told them to get the horses ready. While they were putting them in I fell asleep, and when I woke again I was completely recovered. Yesterday the same thing happened, but in a much less degree."

The palace of illusion, so laboriously raised by the love of the wife, was tottering. In the spiritual blank which followed the achievement of *War and Peace* the artist was recaptured by his philosophical [1] and educational preoccupations ; he wished to write a spelling-book for the people ; he worked at it feverishly for four years ; he was prouder of it than of *War and Peace,* and when it was finished (1872) he wrote a second (1875). Then he conceived a passion for Greek ; he studied Latin from morning to night ; he abandoned all other work ; he discovered " the delightful Xenophon," and Homer, the real Homer ; not the Homer of the translators, " all these Joukhovskys and Vosses who sing with any sort of voice they can manage to produce, guttural, peevish, mawkish," but " this other devil, who sings at the top of his voice, without it ever entering his head that any one may be listening." [2]

" Without a knowledge of Greek, no education ! I am convinced that until now I knew nothing of all that is truly beautiful and of a simple beauty in human speech."

This is folly, and he admits as much. He goes to school again with such passionate enthusiasm

---

[1] While he was finishing *War and Peace,* in the summer of 1869, he discovered Schopenhauer, and was filled with enthusiasm. "I am convinced that Schopenhauer is the most genial of men. Here is the whole universe reflected with an extraordinary clearness and beauty." (Letter to Fet, August 30, 1869.)

[2] Between Homer and his translators," he says again, "there is the difference between boiled and distilled water and the spring-water broken on the rocks, which may carry the sand along with it as it flows, but becomes more pure and fresh on that account."

that he falls ill. In 1871 he was forced to go to Samara to undergo the *koumiss* cure, staying with the Bachkirs. Nothing pleased him but his Greek. At the end of a lawsuit, in 1872, he spoke seriously of selling all that he possessed in Russia and of settling in England. Countess Tolstoy was in despair:

"If you are always absorbed in your Greeks you will never get well. It is they who have caused this suffering and this indifference concerning your present life. It is not in vain that we call Greek a dead language; it produces a condition of death in the spirit."[1]

Finally, to the great joy of the Countess, after many plans abandoned before they were fairly commenced, on March 19, 1873, he began to write *Anna Karenin*.[2] While he worked at it his life was saddened by domestic sorrow;[3] his wife was ill. "Happiness does not reign in the house,"[4] he writes to Fet in 1876.

To some extent the work bears traces of these depressing experiences, and of passions disillusioned.[5] Save in the charming passages dealing

[1] Papers of Countess Tolstoy (*Vie et Œuvre*).

[2] It was completed in 1877. It appeared—minus the epilogue—in the *Rousski Viestniki*.

[3] The death of three children (November 18, 1873, February, 1875, November, 1875); of his Aunt Tatiana, his adopted mother (June, 1874), and of his Aunt Pelagia (December, 1875).

[4] Letter to Fet, March, 1876.

[5] "Woman is the stumbling-block of a man's career. It is difficult to love a woman and to do nothing of any profit; and the only way of not being reduced to inaction by love is to marry." (*Anna Karenin*.)

with the betrothal of Levine, love is no longer
presented with the spirit of youth and poetry
which places certain pages of *War and Peace* on
a level with the most beautiful lyric poetry of all
times. It has assumed a different character : bitter,
sensual, imperious. The fatality which broods over
the romance is no longer, as in *War and Peace*,
a kind of Krishna, murderous and serene, the
Destiny of empires, but the madness of love,
"Venus herself." She it is, in the wonderful ball
scene, when passion seizes upon Anna and Vronsky
unawares, who endows the innocent beauty of Anna,
crowned with forget-me-not and clothed in black
velvet, with "an almost infernal seductiveness." She
it is who, when Vronsky has just declared his love,
throws a light upon Anna's face ; but a light
"not of joy ; it was the terrible glare of an in-
cendiary fire upon a gloomy night." She it is
who, in the veins of this loyal and reasonable
woman, this young, affectionate mother, pours a
voluptuous stream as of irresistible ichor, and in-
stalls herself in her heart, never to leave it until
she has destroyed it. No one can approach Anna
without feeling the attraction and the terror of
this hidden dæmon. Kitty is the first to discover
it, with a shock of bewilderment. A mysterious
fear mingles with the delight of Vronsky when he
goes to see Anna. Levine, in her presence, loses
all his will. Anna herself is perfectly well aware
that she is no longer her own mistress. As the
story develops the implacable passion consumes,
little by little, the whole moral structure of this

proud woman. All that is best in her, her sincere, courageous mind, crumbles and falls; she has no longer the strength to sacrifice her worldly vanity; her life has no other object than to please her lover; she refuses, with shame and terror, to bear children; jealousy tortures her; the sensual passion which enslaves her obliges her to lie with her gestures, her voice, her eyes; she falls to the level of those women who no longer seek anything but the power of making every man turn to look after them; she uses morphia to dull her sufferings, until the intolerable torments which consume her overcome her with the bitter sense of her moral downfall, and cast her beneath the wheels of the railway-carriage. "And the little moujik with the untidy beard" — the sinister vision which has haunted her dreams and Vronsky's—"leaned over the track from the platform of the carriage"; and, as the prophetic dream foretold, "he was bent double over a sack, in which he was hiding the remains of something which had known life, with its torments, its betrayals, and its sorrows."

"Vengeance is mine, saith the Lord."[1]

Around this tragedy of a soul consumed by love and crushed by the law of God—a painting in a single shade, and of terrible gloom—Tolstoy has woven, as in *War and Peace*, the romances of other lives. Unfortunately these parallel stories alternate in a somewhat stiff and artificial manner, without achieving the organic unity of the symphony of

[1] The motto at the commencement of the book.

War and Peace. It may also be said that the perfect realism of certain of the pictures—the aristocratic circles of St. Petersburg and their idle discourse—is now and again superfluous and unnecessary. Finally, and more openly than in *War and Peace,* Tolstoy has presented his own moral character and his philosophic ideas side by side with the spectacle of life. None the less, the work is of a marvellous richness. There is the same profusion of types as in *War and Peace,* and all are of a striking justness. The portraits of the men seem to me even superior. Tolstoy has depicted with evident delight the amiable egoist, Stepan Arcadievitch, whom no one can look at without responding to his affectionate smile, and Karenin, the perfect type of the high official, the distinguished and commonplace statesman, with his mania for concealing his real opinions and feelings under a mask of perpetual irony : a mixture of dignity and cowardice, of Phariseeism and Christian feeling : a strange product of an artificial world, from which he can never completely free himself in spite of his intelligence and his true generosity ; a man afraid to listen to his own heart, and rightly so afraid, since when he does surrender to it, he ends by falling into a state of nonsensical mysticism.

But the principal interest of the romance, besides the tragedy of Anna and the varied pictures of Russian society towards 1860—of salons, officers' clubs, balls, theatres, races — lies in its autobiographical character. More than any other

personage of Tolstoy's books, Constantine Levine
is the incarnation of the writer himself. Not only
has Tolstoy attributed to him his own ideas—at one
and the same time conservative and democratic—
and the anti-Liberalism of the provincial aristocrat
who despises "intellectuals"; [1] but he has made
him the gift of part of his own life. The love of
Levine and Kitty and their first years of marriage
are a transposition of his own domestic memories,
just as the death of Levine's brother is a melancholy
evocation of the death of Tolstoy's brother, Dmitri.
The latter portion, useless to the romance, gives us
an insight into the troubles which were then oppress-
ing the author. While the epilogue of *War and
Peace* was an artistic transition to another projected work, the epilogue to *Anna Karenin* is an
autobiographical transition to the moral revolution
which, two years later, was to find expression in
the *Confessions*. Already, in the course of *Anna
Karenin*, he returns again and again to a violent
or ironical criticism of contemporary society, which
he never ceased to attack in his subsequent works.
War is declared upon deceit : war upon lies ; upon
virtuous as well as vicious lies ; upon liberal
chatter, fashionable charity, drawing-room religion,
and philanthropy. War against the world, which
distorts all truthful feelings, and `inevitably crushes
the generous enthusiasm of the mind ! Death
throws an unexpected light upon the social conventions. Before Anna dying, the stilted Karenin

[1] Notice also, in the epilogue, the hostility towards warfare,
nationalism, and Pan-Slavism.

is softened. Into this lifeless soul, in which everything is artificial, shines a ray of love and of
Christian forgiveness. All three — the husband,
the wife, and the lover—are momentarily trans-
formed. All three become simple and loyal. But
as Anna recovers, all three are sensible, "facing
the almost holy moral strength which was guiding
them from within, the existence of another force,
brutal but all-powerful, which was directing their
lives despite themselves, and which would not
leave them in peace." And they knew from the
beginning that they would be powerless in the
coming struggle, in which "they would be obliged
to do the evil that the world would consider
necessary." [1]

If Levine, like Tolstoy, whose incarnation he is,
also became purified in the epilogue to the book, it
was because he too was touched by mortality.
Previously, "incapable of believing, he was equally
incapable of absolute doubt." [2] After he beheld his
brother die the terror of his ignorance possessed
him. For a time this misery was stifled by his
marriage ; but it re-awakened at the birth of his
firstborn. He passed alternately through crises
of prayer and negation. He read the philosophers
in vain. He began, in his distracted state, to fear
the temptation of suicide. Physical work was a
solace ; it presented no doubts ; all was clear.
Levine conversed with the peasants ; one of them

---

[1] "Evil is that which is reasonable to the world. Sacrifice
and love are insanity." (*Anna Karenin*, vol. ii.)

[2] *Anna Karenin*, vol. ii.

spoke of the men " who live not for self, but for God." This was to him an illumination. He saw the antagonism between the reason and the heart. Reason preached the ferocious struggle for life ; there is nothing reasonable in loving one's neighbour :

" Reason has taught me nothing ; all that I know has been given to me, revealed to me by the heart." [1]

From this time peace returned. The word of the humble peasant, whose heart was his only guide, had led him back to God. . . . To what God ? He did not seek to know. His attitude toward the Church at this moment, as was Tolstoy's for a long period, was humble, and in no wise defiant of her dogmas.

" There is a truth even in the illusion of the celestial vault and in the apparent movement of the stars." [2]

[1] *Anna Karenin*, vol. ii.   [2] *Ibid.*

X

THE CRISIS

CHAPTER X

THE CRISIS

THE misery which oppressed Levine, and the long-
ing for suicide which he concealed from Kitty,
Tolstoy was at this period concealing from his wife.
But he had not as yet achieved the calm which he
attributed to his hero. To be truthful, this mental
state is hardly communicated to the reader. We
feel that it is desired rather than realised, and that
Levine's relapse among his doubts is imminent.
Tolstoy was not duped by his desires. He had the
greatest difficulty in reaching the end of his work.
Anna Karenin wearied him before he had finished
it.[1] He could work no longer. He remained at a
standstill ; inert, without will-power, a prey to self-
terror and self-disgust. There, in the emptiness of
his life, rose the great wind which issued from the
abyss ; the vertigo of death.

Tolstoy told of these terrible years at a later

[1] "Now I am harnessing myself again to the wearisome and
vulgar *Anna Karenin*, with the sole desire of getting rid of it
as quickly as possible." (Letters to Fet, August 26, 1875.) "I
must finish the romance, which is wearying me." (*Ibid.*
March 1, 1876.)

period, when he was newly escaped from the abyss.[1]

"I was not fifty," he said; "I loved; I was loved; I had good children, a great estate, fame, health, and moral and physical vigour; I could reap or mow like any peasant; I used to work ten hours at a stretch without fatigue. Suddenly my life came to a standstill. I could breathe, eat, drink and sleep. But this was not to live. I had no desires left. I knew there was nothing to desire. I could not even wish to know the truth. The truth was that life is a piece of insanity. I had reached the abyss, and I saw clearly that there was nothing before me but death. I, a fortunate and healthy man, felt that I could not go on living. An irresistible force was urging me to rid myself of life. . . . I will not say that I wanted to kill myself. The force which was edging me out of life was something stronger than myself; it was an aspiration, a desire like my old desire for life, but in an inverse sense. I had to humour, to deceive myself, lest I should give way to it too promptly. There I was, a happy man, —and I would hide away a piece of cord lest I should hang myself from the beam that ran between the cupboards of my room, where I was alone every night while undressing. I no longer took my gun out for a little shooting, lest I should be tempted.[2]

[1] In his *Confessions* (1879).

[2] See *Anna Karenin*. "And Levine, who had the love of a woman, and was the father of a family, put every kind of weapon away out of reach, as though he was afraid of yielding to the temptation of putting an end to his sufferings."

It seemed to me that life was a dreary farce, which was being played out before my eyes. Forty years of work, of trouble, of progress, only to find that there is nothing ! Nothing ! Nothing will remain of me but putrescence and worms. . . . One can live only while one is intoxicated with life ; but the moment the intoxication is over one sees that all is merely deceit, a clumsy fraud. . . . My family and art were no longer enough to satisfy me. My family consisted of unhappy creatures like myself. Art is a mirror to life. When life no longer means anything it is no longer amusing to use the mirror. And the worst of it was, I could not resign myself— I was like a man lost in a forest, who is seized with horror because he is lost, and who runs hither and thither and cannot stop, although he knows that at every step he is straying further."

Salvation came from the people. Tolstoy had always had for them " a strange affection, absolutely genuine," [1] which the repeated experiences of his social disillusions were powerless to shake. Of late years he, like Levine, had drawn

This frame of mind was not peculiar to Tolstoy and his characters. Tolstoy was struck by the increasing number of suicides among the wealthy classes all over Europe, and in Russia more especially. He often alludes to the fact in such of his books as were written about this period. It was as though a great wave of neurasthenia had swept across Europe in 1880, drowning its thousands of victims. Those who were young men at the time will remember it ; and for them Tolstoy's record of this human experience will have a historic value. He has written the secret tragedy of a generation.

[1] *Confessions.*

very near to them.[1]   He began to ponder concerning these millions of beings who were excluded from the narrow circle of the learned, the rich, and the idle who killed themselves, endeavoured to forget themselves, or, like himself, were basely prolonging a hopeless life.   He asked himself why these millions of men and women escaped this despair : why they did not kill themselves.   He then perceived that they were living not by the light of reason, but without even thinking of reason ; they were living by faith.   What was this faith which knew nothing of reason ?

"Faith is the energy of life.   One cannot live without faith.   The ideas of religion were elaborated in the infinite remoteness of human thought.   The replies given by faith to Life the sphinx contain the deepest wisdom of humanity."

Is it enough, then, to be acquainted with those formulæ of wisdom recorded in the volume of religion ?   No, for faith is not a science ; faith is an act ; it has no meaning unless it is lived.   The disgust which Tolstoy felt at the sight of rich and *rightthinking* people, for whom faith was merely a kind

---

[1] His portraits of this period betray this plebeian tendency. A painting by Kramskoy (1873) represents Tolstoy in a moujik's blouse, with bowed head : it resembles a German Christ.   The forehead is growing bare at the temples ; the cheeks are lined and bearded.—In another portrait, dated 1881, he has the look of a respectable artisan in his Sunday clothes : the hair cut short, the beard and whiskers spread out on either side ; the face looks much wider below than above ; the eyebrows are contracted, the eyes gloomy ; the wide nostrils have a dog-like appearance ; the ears are enormous.

of "epicurean consolation," threw him definitely among the simple folk who alone lived lives in agreement with their faith.

"And he understood that the life of the labouring people was life itself, and that the meaning to be attributed to that life was truth."

But how become a part of the people and share its faith ? It is not enough to know that others are in the right; it does not depend upon ourselves whether we are like them. We pray to God in vain; in vain we stretch our eager arms toward Him. God flies. Where shall He be found ?

But one day grace descended :

"One day of early spring I was alone in the forest, listening to its sounds. . . . I was thinking of my distress during the last three years ; of my search for God ; of my perpetual oscillations from joy to despair. . . . And I suddenly saw that I used to live only when I used to believe in God. At the very thought of Him the delightful waves of life stirred in me. Everything around me grew full of life ; everything received a meaning. But the moment I no longer believed life suddenly ceased.

"Then what am I still searching for ? a voice cried within me. For Him, without whom man cannot live ! To know God and to live—it is the same thing ! For God is Life. . . . .

"Since then this light has never again deserted me." [1]

[1] *Confessions.*

He was saved. God had appeared to him.[1]

But as he was not a Hindu mystic, to whom ecstasy suffices ; as to the dreams of the Asiatic was added the thirst for reason and the need of action of the Occidental, he was moved to translate his revelation into terms of practical faith, and to draw from the holy life the rules of daily existence. Without any previous bias, and sincerely wishing to believe in the beliefs of his own flesh and blood,

---

[1] To tell the truth—not for the first time. The young volunteer in the Caucasus, the officer at Sebastopol, Olenin of the *Cossacks*, Prince Andrei, and Pierre Besoukhov, in *War and Peace*, had had similar visions. But Tolstoy was so enthusiastic that each time he discovered God he believed it was for the first time ; that previously there had been nothing but night and the void. He saw nothing of his past but its shadows and its shames. We who, through reading his *Journal*, know better than he himself the story of his heart, know also how profoundly religious was that heart, even when he was most astray. But he himself confesses in a passage in the preface to the *Criticism of Dogmatic Theology :* "God ! God ! I have erred ; I have sought the truth where I should not have sought it ; and I knew that I erred. I flattered my evil passions, knowing them to be evil ; *but I never forgot Thee. I was always conscious of Thee, even when I went astray."* The crisis of 1878–79 was only more violent than the rest ; perhaps under the influence of repeated loss and the advance of age ; its only novelty was that the image of God, instead of vanishing and leaving no trace when once the flame of ecstasy flickered out, remained with him, and the penitent, warned by past experience, hastened to "walk in the light while he had the light," and to deduce from his faith a whole system of life. Not that he had not already tried to do so. (Remember the *Rules of Life* written when he was a student.) But at fifty years of age there was less likelihood that his passions would divert him from his path.

he began by studying the doctrine of the Orthodox Church, of which he was a member.[1] In order to become more intimately a part of that body he submitted for three years to all its ceremonies; confessing himself, communicating; not presuming to judge such matters as shocked him, inventing explanations for what he found obscure or incomprehensible, uniting himself, through and in their faith, with all those whom he loved, whether living or dead, and always cherishing the hope that at a certain moment "love would open to him the gates of truth." But it was all useless: his reason and his heart revolted. Such ceremonies as baptism and communion appeared to him scandalous. When he was forced to repeat that the host was the true body and true blood of Christ, "he felt as though a knife were plunged into his heart." But it was not the dogmas which raised between the Church and himself an insurmountable wall, but the practical questions, and in especial two: the hateful and mutual intolerance of the Churches[2] and the sanction, formal or tacit, of homicide: of war and of capital punishment.

So he broke loose, and the rupture was the more violent in that for three years he had suppressed his faculty of thought. He walked delicately no

[1] The sub-title of the *Confessions* is *Introduction to the Criticism of Dogmatic Theology and the Examination of the Christian Doctrine.*

[2] "I, who beheld the truth in the unity of love, was struck with the fact that religion itself destroyed that which it sought to produce." (*Confessions.*)

longer. Angrily and violently he trampled underfoot the religion which the day before he was
still persistently practising. In his *Criticism of
Dogmatic Theology* (1879–1881) he termed it not
only an "insanity, but a conscious and interested
lie."[1] He contrasted it with the New Testament,
in his *Concordance and Translation of the Four
Gospels* (1881–83). Finally, upon the Gospel he
built his faith (*What my Faith consists in*, 1883).

It all resides in these words :

"I believe in the doctrine of the Christ. I
believe that happiness is possible on earth only
when all men shall accomplish it."

Its corner-stone is the Sermon on the Mount,
whose essential teaching Tolstoy expresses in five
commandments :

"1. Do not be angry.

"2. Do not commit adultery.

"3. Do not take oaths.

"4. Do not resist evil by evil.

"5. Be no man's enemy."

This is the negative part of the doctrine ; the
positive portion is contained in this single commandment :

"Love God, and thy neighbour as thyself."

"Christ has said that he who shall have broken
the least of these commandments will hold the
lowest place in the kingdom of heaven."

[1] "And I am convinced that the teaching of the Church is
in theory a crafty and evil lie, and in practice a concoction
of gross superstitions and witchcraft, under which the meaning of the Christian doctrine absolutely disappears." (*Reply
to the Holy Synod*, April 4–17, 1901.)

And Tolstoy adds naïvely :

"Strange as it may seem, I have been obliged, after eighteen centuries, to discover these rules as a novelty."

Does Tolstoy believe in the divinity of Christ ? By no means. In what quality does he invoke him ? As the greatest of the line of sages— Brahma, Buddha, Lao-Tse, Confucius, Zoroaster, Isaiah—who have revealed to man the true happiness to which he aspires, and the way which he must follow.[1] Tolstoy is the disciple of these great religious creators, of these Hindu, Chinese, and Hebrew demi-gods and prophets. He defends

[1] As he grew older, this feeling of the unity of religious truth throughout human history—and of the kinship of Christ with the other sages, from Buddha down to Kant and Emerson —grew more and more accentuated, until in his later years Tolstoy denied that he had "any predilection for Christianity." Of the greatest importance in this connection is a letter written between July 27 and August 4, 1909, to the painter Jan Styka, and recently reproduced in *Le Théosophe* (January 16, 1911). According to his habit, Tolstoy, full of his new conviction, was a little inclined to forget his former state of mind and the starting-point of his religious crisis, which was purely Christian :

"The doctrine of Jesus," he writes, "is to me only one of the beautiful doctrines which we have received from the ancient civilisations of Egypt, Israel, Hindostan, China, Greece. The two great principles of Jesus : the love of God, that is, of absolute perfection, and the love of one's neighbour, that is, of all men without distinction, have been preached by all the sages of the world : Krishna, Buddha, Lao-Tse, Confucius, Socrates, Plato, Epictetus, Marcus Aurelius, and, among the moderns, Rousseau, Pascal, Kant, Emerson, Channing, and many others. Truth, moral and religious, is everywhere and always the same. . . . I have no predilection

them, as he knows how to defend ; defends them
by attacking those whom he calls "the Scribes"
and "the Pharisees" ; by attacking the established
Churches and the representatives of arrogant science,
or rather of "scientific philosophism." Not that
he appealed from reason to revelation. Once
escaped from the period of distress described in his
Confessions, he remained essentially a believer in
Reason ; one might indeed say a mystic of Reason.

"In the beginning was the Word," he says, with
St. John ; "the Word, Logos, that is, Reason." [1]

A book of his entitled *Life* (1887) bears as
epigraph the famous lines of Pascal : [2]

"Man is nothing but a reed, the most feeble
thing in nature, but he is a thinking reed. . . . All
our dignity resides in thought. . . . Let us then
strive to think well : that is the principle of
morality."

The whole book, moreover, is nothing but a
hymn to Reason.

It is true that Tolstoy's Reason is not the scientific reason, the restricted reason "which takes the

for Christianity. If I have been particularly attracted by the
teaching of Jesus, it is (1) because I was born and have lived
among Christians, and (2) because I have found a great
spiritual joy in disengaging the pure doctrine from the
astonishing falsifications created by the Churches."

[1] Tolstoy protests that he does not attack true science,
which is modest and knows its limits. (*Life*, chap. iv. There
is a French version by Countess Tolstoy.)

[2] Tolstoy often read the *Pensées* during the period of this
crisis, which preceded the *Confessions*. He speaks of Pascal
in his letters to Fet (April 14, 1877, August 3, 1879), recom-
mending his friend to read the *Pensées*.

part for the whole and physical life for the whole of life," but the sovereign law which rules the life of man, "the law according to which *reasonable beings, that is men,* must of necessity live their lives."

"It is a law analogous to those which regulate the nutrition and the reproduction of the animal, the growth and the blossoming of herb and of tree, the movement of the earth and the planets. It is only in the accomplishment of this law, in the submission of our animal nature to the law of reason, with a view to acquiring goodness, that we truly live. . . . Reason cannot be defined, and we have no need to define it, for not only do we all know it, but we know nothing else. . . . All that man knows he knows by means of reason and not by faith. . . .[1] True life commences only at the moment when reason is manifested. The only real life is the life of reason."

Then what is the visible life, our individual existence ? "It is not our life," says Tolstoy, "for it does not depend upon ourselves.

"Our animal activity is accomplished without ourselves. . . . Humanity has done with the idea of life considered as an individual existence. The

[1] In a letter *Upon Reason,* written on November 26, 1894, to Baroness X (reproduced in *The Revolutionaries,* 1906), Tolstoy says the same thing :

"Man has received directly from God one sole instrument by which he may know himself and his relations with the world : there is no other means. This instrument is reason. Reason comes from God. It is not only the highest human quality, but the only means by which the truth is to be known."

negation of the possibility of individual good
remains an unchangeable truth for every man of
our period who is endowed with reason."

Then follows a long series of postulates, which
I will not here discuss, but which show how
Tolstoy was obsessed by the idea of reason. It
was in fact a passion, no less blind or jealous
than the other passions which had possessed him
during the earlier part of his life. One fire was
flickering out, the other was kindling; or rather it
was always the same fire, but fed with a different
fuel.

A fact which adds to the resemblance between
the "individual" passions and this "rational"
passion is that neither those nor this can be satisfied
with loving. They seek to act; they long for
realisation.

"Christ has said, we must not speak, but act."

And what is the activity of reason ?—Love.

"Love is the only reasonable activity of man;
love is the most reasonable and most enlightened
state of the soul. All that man needs is that nothing
shall obscure the sun of reason, for that alone can
help him to grow. . . . Love is the actual good, the
supreme good which resolves all the contradictions
of life; which not only dissipates the fear of death,
but impels man to sacrifice himself to others : for
there is no love but that which enables a man to
give his life for those he loves : love is not worthy
of the name unless it is a sacrifice of self. And the
true love can only be realised when man understands that it is not possible for him to acquire

individual happiness.   It is then that all the streams
of his life go to nourish the noble graft of the true
love : and this graft borrows for its increase all the
energies of the wild stock of animal individu-
ality. . . ." [1]

Thus Tolstoy did not come to the refuge of
faith like an exhausted river which loses itself
among the sands.   He brought to it the torrent of
impetuous energies amassed during a full and
virile life.   This we shall presently see.

This impassioned faith, in which Love and
Reason are united in a close embrace, has found
its most dignified expression in the famous reply
to the Holy Synod which excommunicated him : [2]

" I believe in God, who for me is Love, the Spirit,
the Principle of all things.   I believe that He is in
me as I am in Him.   I believe that the will of God
has never been more clearly expressed than in the
teaching of the man Christ ; but we cannot regard
Christ as God and address our prayers to him without committing the greatest sacrilege.   I believe
that the true happiness of man consists in the
accomplishment of the will of God ; I believe that
the will of God is that every man shall love his
fellows and do unto them always as he would they
should do unto him, which contains, as the Bible

---

[1] *Life*, xxii.–xxv.   As in the case of most of these quo-
tations, I am expressing the sense of several chapters in a few
characteristic phrases.

[2] I hope later, when the complete works of Tolstoy have
been published, to study the various shades of this religious
idea, which has certainly evolved in respect of many points,
notably in respect of the conception of future life.

says, all the law and the prophets. I believe that the meaning of life for each one of us is only to increase the love within him; I believe that this development of our power of loving will reward us in this life with a happiness which will increase day by day, and with a more perfect felicity in the other world. I believe that this increase of love will contribute, more than any other factor, to founding the kingdom of God upon earth; that is, to replacing an organisation of life in which division, deceit, and violence are omnipotent, by a new order in which concord, truth, and brotherhood will reign. I believe that we have only one means of growing richer in love: namely, our prayers. Not public prayer in the temple, which Christ has formally reproved (Matt. vi. 5–13), but the prayer of which he himself has given as an example; the solitary prayer which confirms in us the consciousness of the meaning of our life and the feeling that we depend solely upon the will of God. . . . I believe in life eternal; I believe that man is rewarded according to his acts, here and everywhere, now and for ever. I believe all these things so firmly that at my age, on the verge of the tomb, I have often to make an effort not to pray for the death of my body, that is, my birth into a new life." [1]

[1] From a translation in the *Temps* for May 1, 1901.

XI

REALITY

CHAPTER XI

REALITY

HE thought he had arrived in port, had achieved the haven in which his unquiet soul might take its repose. He was only at the beginning of a new period of activity.

A winter passed in Moscow (his family duties having obliged him to follow his family thither),[1] and the taking of the census, in which he contrived to lend a hand, gave him the occasion to examine at first hand the poverty of a great city. The impression produced upon him was terrible. On the evening of the day when he first came into contact with this hidden plague of civilisation, while relating to a friend what he had seen, "he began to shout, to weep, and to brandish his fist."

"People can't live like that !" he cried, sobbing. "It cannot be ! It cannot be !" He fell into a state of terrible despair, which did not leave him for months. Countess Tolstoy wrote to him on the 3rd of March, 1882 :

[1] "I had hitherto passed my whole life away from the city." (*What shall we do ?*)

"You used to say, 'I used to want to hang myself because of my lack of faith.' Now you have faith : why then are you so unhappy ?"

Because he had not the sanctimonious, self-satisfied faith of the Pharisee ; because he had not the egoism of the mystic, who is too completely absorbed in the matter of his own salvation to think of the salvation of others" ; [1] because he knew love ; because he could no longer forget the miserable creatures he had seen, and in the passionate tenderness of his heart he felt as though he were responsible for their sufferings and their abjectness ; they were the victims of that civilisation in whose privileges he shared ; of that monstrous idol to which an elect and superior class was always sacrificing millions of human beings. To accept the benefit of such crimes was to become an accomplice. His conscience would have given him no repose had he not denounced them.

[1] Tolstoy has many times expressed his antipathy for the "ascetics, who live for themselves only, apart from their fellows." He puts them in the same class as the conceited and ignorant revolutionists, "who pretend to do good to others without knowing what it is that they themselves need. . . . I love these two categories of men with the same love, but I hate their doctrines with the same hate. The only doctrine is that which orders a constant activity, an existence which responds to the aspirations of the soul and endeavours to realise the happiness of others. Such is the Christian doctrine. Equally remote from religious quietism and the arrogant pretensions of the revolutionists, who seek to transform the world without knowing in what real happiness consists." (Letters to a friend, published in the volume entitled *Cruel Pleasures*, 1895.)

What shall we do? (1884–86) is the expression
of this second crisis ; a crisis far more tragic than
the first, and far richer in consequences. What
were the personal religious sufferings of Tolstoy
in this ocean of human wretchedness—of material
misery, not misery created by the mind of a self-
wearied idler ? It was impossible for him to shut
his eyes to it, and having seen it he could but strive,
at any cost, to prevent it. Alas ! was such a thing
possible ?

An admirable portrait,[1] which I cannot look at
without emotion, tells us plainly what suffering
Tolstoy was then enduring. It shows him facing the
camera ; seated, with his arms crossed ; he is wear-
a moujik's blouse. He looks overwhelmed. His
hair is still black, but his moustache is already grey,
and his long beard and whiskers are quite white.
A double furrow traces symmetrical lines in the
large, comely face. There is so much goodness,
such tenderness, in the great dog-like muzzle, in the
eyes that regard you with so frank, so clear, so
sorrowful a look. They read your mind so surely !
They pity and implore. The face is furrowed and
bears traces of suffering ; there are heavy creases
beneath the eyes. He has wept. But he is strong,
and ready for the fight.

His logic was heroic :

"I am always astonished by these words, so
often repeated : ' Yes, it is well enough in theory,
but how would it be in practice ?" As if theory

[1] A daguerreotype of 1885, reproduced in *What shall we
do ?* in the complete French edition.

consisted in pretty words, necessary for conversation, and was not in the least something to which practice should conform ! When I come to understand a matter on which I have reflected, I cannot do otherwise than as I have understood."[1]

He begins by describing, with photographic exactitude, the poverty of Moscow as he has seen it in the course of his visits to the poorer quarters or the night-shelters.[2]

He is convinced that money is not the power, as he had at first supposed, which will save these unhappy creatures, all more or less tainted by the corruption of the cities. Then he seeks bravely for the source of the evil ; unwinding link upon link of the terrible chain of responsibility. First come the rich, with the contagion of their accursed luxury, which entices and depraves the soul.[3] Then comes the universal seduction of life without labour. Then the State, that murderous entity, created by the violent in order that they might for their own profit despoil and enslave the rest of humanity. Then the Church, an accomplice ; science and art, accomplices. How is a man to oppose this army of evil ? In the first place, by refusing to

---

[1] *What shall we do ?*

[2] All the first part of the book (the first fifteen chapters).

[3] "The true cause of poverty is the accumulation of riches in the hands of those who do not produce, and are concentrated in the cities. The wealthy classes are gathered together in the cities in order to enjoy and to defend themselves. And the poor man comes to feed upon the crumbs of the rich. He is drawn thither by the snare of easy gain : by peddling, begging, swindling, or in the service of immorality."

join it. By refusing to share in the exploitation of humanity. By renouncing wealth and ownership of the soil,[1] and by refusing to serve the State.

But this is not sufficient. One "must not lie," nor be afraid of the truth. One "must repent," and uproot the pride that is implanted by education. Finally, one must work with one's hands. "*Thou shalt win thy bread in the sweat of thy brow*" is the first commandment and the most essential.[2] And Tolstoy, replying in advance to the ridicule of the elect, maintains that physical labour does not in any way decrease the energy of the intellect ; but that, on the contrary, it increases it, and that it responds to the normal demand of nature. Health can only

[1] "The pivot of the evil is property. Property is merely the means of enjoying the labour of others." Property, he says again, is that which is not ours: it represents other people. "Man calls his wife, his children, his slaves, his goods his property, but reality shows him his error ; and he must renounce his property or suffer and cause others to suffer."

Tolstoy was already urging the Russian revolution : " For three or four years now men have cursed us on the highway and called us sluggards and skulkers. The hatred and contempt of the downtrodden people are becoming more intense." (*What shall we do ?*)

[2] The peasant-revolutionist Bondarev would have had this law recognised as a universal obligation. Tolstoy was then subject to his influence, as also to that of another peasant, Sutayev.—" During the whole of my life two Russian thinkers have had a great moral influence over me, have enriched my mind, and have elucidated for me my own conception of the world. They were two peasants, Sutayev and Bondarev." (*What shall we do ?*)

In the same book Tolstoy gives us a portrait of Sutayev, and records a conversation with him.

gain thereby ; art will gain even more. But what is more important still, it will re-establish the union of man with man.

In his subsequent works, Tolstoy was to complete these precepts of moral hygiene. He was anxious to achieve the cure of the soul, to replenish its energy, by proscribing the vicious pleasures which deaden the conscience[1] and the cruel pleasures which kill it.[2] He himself set the example. In 1884, he sacrificed his most deeply rooted passion : his love of the chase.[3] He practised abstinence, which strengthens the will. So an athlete may subject himself to some painful discipline that he may grapple with it and conquer.

What shall we do ? marks the first stage of the difficult journey upon which Tolstoy was about to embark, quitting the relative peace of religious meditation for the social maëlstrom. It was then that the twenty years' war commenced which the old prophet of Yasnaya Polyana waged in the name of the Gospel, single-handed, outside the limits of all parties, and condemning all ; a war upon the crimes and lies of civilisation.

---

[1] *Vicious Pleasures*, or in the French translation *Alcohol and Tobacco*, 1895.

[2] *Cruel Pleasures* (*the Meat-eaters ; War ; Hunting*), 1895.

[3] The sacrifice was difficult ; the passion inherited. He was not sentimental ; he never felt much pity for animals. For him all things fell into three planes : " 1. Reasoning beings ; 2. animals and plants ; 3. inanimate matter." He was not without a trace of native cruelty. He relates the pleasure he felt in watching the struggles of a wolf which he killed. Remorse was of later growth.

XII

ART AND
CONSCIENCE

CHAPTER XII

ART AND CONSCIENCE

THIS moral revolution of Tolstoy's met with little sympathy from his immediate world; his family and his relatives were appalled by it.

For a long time Countess Tolstoy had been anxiously watching the progress of a symptom against which she had fought in vain. As early as 1874 she had seen with indignation the amount of time and energy which her husband spent in connection with the schools.

"This spelling-book, this arithmetic, this grammar —I feel a contempt for them, and I cannot assume a semblance of interest in them."

Matters were very different when pedagogy was succeeded by religion. So hostile was the Countess's reception of the first confidences of the convert that Tolstoy felt obliged to apologise when he spoke of God in his letters :

" Do not be vexed, as you so often are when I mention God ; I cannot help it, for He is the very basis of my thought." [1]

[1] The summer of 1878.

The Countess was touched, no doubt; she tried to conceal her impatience; but she did not understand; and she watched her husband anxiously.

"His eyes are strange and fixed. He scarcely speaks. He does not seem to belong to this world."

She feared he was ill.

"Leo is always working, by what he tells me. Alas! he is writing religious discussions of some kind. He reads and he ponders until he gives himself the headache, and all this to prove that the Church is not in agreement with the teaching of the Gospel. He will hardly find a dozen people in Russia whom the matter could possibly interest. But there is nothing to be done. I have only one hope: that he will be done with it all the sooner, and that it will pass off like an illness."

The illness did not pass away. The situation between husband and wife became more and more painful. They loved one another; each had a profound esteem for the other; but it was impossible for them to understand one another. They strove to make mutual concessions, which became—as is usually the case—a form of mutual torment. Tolstoy forced himself to follow his family to Moscow. He wrote in his *Journal*:

"The most painful month of my life. Getting settled in Moscow. All are settling down. But when, then, will they begin to live? All this, not in order to live, but because other folk do the same. Unhappy people!"[1]

During these days the Countess wrote:

[1] October 8, 1881. *Vie et Œuvre.*

" Moscow. We shall have been here a month to-morrow. The first two weeks I cried every day, for Leo was not only sad, but absolutely broken. He did not sleep, he did not eat, at times even he wept ; I thought I should go mad." [1]

For a time they had to live their lives apart. They begged one another's pardon for causing mutual suffering. We see how they always loved each other. He writes to her :

" You say, ' I love you, and you do not need my love.' It is the only thing I do need. . . . Your love causes me more gladness than anything in the world."

But as soon as they are together again the same discord occurs. The Countess cannot share this religious mania which is now impelling Tolstoy to study Hebrew with a rabbi.

" Nothing else interests him any longer. He is wasting his energies in foolishness. I cannot conceal my impatience." [2]

She writes to him :

" It can only sadden me that such intellectual energies should spend themselves in chopping wood, heating the samovar, and cobbling boots."

She adds, with affectionate, half-ironical humour of a mother who watches a child playing a foolish game :

" Finally, I have pacified myself with the Russian proverb : ' Let the child play as he will, so long as he doesn't cry.' " [3]

[1] October 14. *Vie et Œuvre.*   [2] 1882.
[3] October 23, 1884. *Vie et Œuvre.*

Before the letter was posted she had a mental vision of her husband reading these lines, his kind, frank eyes saddened by their ironical tone ; and she re-opened the letter, in an impulse of affection :

" Quite suddenly I saw you so clearly, and I felt such a rush of tenderness for you ! There is something in you so wise, so naïve, so persevering, and it is all lit up by the radiance of goodness, and that look of yours which goes straight to the soul. . . . It is something that belongs to you alone."

In this manner these two creatures who loved also tormented one another and were straightway stricken with wretchedness because of the pain they had the power to inflict but not the power to avoid. A situation with no escape, which lasted for nearly thirty years ; which was to be terminated only by the flight across the steppes, in a moment of aberration, of the ancient Lear, with death already upon him.

Critics have not sufficiently remarked the moving appeal to women which terminates *What shall we do ?* Tolstoy had no sympathy for modern feminism.[1] But of the type whom he calls "the mother-woman," the woman who knows the real meaning of life, he speaks in terms of pious admiration ; he pronounces a magnificent eulogy of her pains and her joys, of pregnancy and maternity, of the terrible

[1] "The so-called right of women is merely the desire to participate in the imaginary labours of the wealthy classes, with a view to enjoying the fruit of the labour of others and to live a life that satisfies the sensual appetites. No genuine labourer's wife demands the right to share her husband's work in the mines or in the fields."

sufferings, the years without rest, the invisible, exhausting travail for which no reward is expected, and of that beatitude which floods the soul at the happy issue from labour, when the body has accomplished the Law. He draws the portrait of the valiant wife who is a help, not an obstacle, to her husband. She knows that "the vocation of man is the obscure, lonely sacrifice, unrewarded, for the life of others."

"Such a woman will not only not encourage her husband in factitious and mericious work whose only end is to profit by and enjoy the labour of others; but she will regard such activity with horror and disgust, as a possible seduction for her children. She will demand of her companion a true labour, which will call for energy and does not fear danger. . . . She knows that the children, the generations to come, are given to men as their holiest vision, and that she exists to further, with all her being, this sacred task. She will develop in her children and in her husband the strength of sacrifice. . . . It is such women who rule men and serve as their guiding star. . . . O mother-women ! In your hands is the salvation of the world !" [1]

This appeal of a voice of supplication, which still has hope—will it not be heard ?

A few years later the last glimmer of hope was dead.

"Perhaps you will not believe me; but you cannot imagine how isolated I am, nor in what a

[1] These are the last lines of *What shall we do ?* They are dated the 14th of February, 1886.

degree my veritable *I* is despised and disregarded by all those about me." [1]

If those who loved him best so misunderstood the grandeur of the moral transformation which Tolstoy was undergoing, one could not look for more penetration or greater respect in others. Tourgenev with whom he had sought to effect a reconciliation, rather in a spirit of Christian humility than because his feelings towards him had suffered any change,[2] said ironically of Tolstoy : " I pity him greatly ; but after all, as the French say, every one kills his own fleas in his own way." [3]

A few years later, when on the point of death, he wrote to Tolstoy the well-known letter in which he prayed "his friend, the great writer of the Russian world," to "return to literature." [4]

All the artists of Europe shared the anxiety and the prayer of the dying Tourgenev. Melchior de Vogüé, at the end of his study of Tolstoy, written in 1886, made a portrait of the writer in peasant costume, handling a drill, the pretext for an eloquent apostrophe :

"Craftsman, maker of masterpieces, this is not

---

[1] A letter to a friend, published under the title *Profession of Faith*, in the volume entitled *Cruel Pleasures*, 1895.

[2] The reconciliation took place in the spring of 1878. Tolstoy wrote to Tourgenev asking his pardon. Tourgenev went to Yasnaya Polyana in August, 1878. Tolstoy returned his visit in July, 1881. Every one was struck with the change in his manner, his gentleness and his modesty. He was "as though regenerated."

[3] Letter to Polonski (quoted by Birukov).

[4] Letter to Bougival June 28, 1883.

your tool! . . . Our tool is the pen; our field, the human soul, which we must shelter and nourish. Let us remind you of the words of a Russian peasant, of the the first printer of Moscow, when he was sent back to the plough : 'It is not my business to sow grains of corn, but to sow the seed of the spirit broadcast in the world.'"

As though Tolstoy had ever renounced his vocation as a sower of the seed of the mind! In the Introduction to *What I Believe* he wrote :

"I believe that my life, my reason, my light, is given me exclusively for the purpose of enlightening my fellows. I believe that my knowledge of the truth is a talent which is lent me for this object; that this talent is a fire which is a fire only when it is being consumed. I believe that the only meaning of my life is that I should live it only by the light within me, and should hold that light on high before men that they may see it."[1]

But this light, this fire "which was a fire only when it was being consumed," was a cause of anxiety to the majority of Tolstoy's fellow-artists. The more intelligent could not but suspect that

[1] We find that M. de Vogüé, in the reproach which he addressed to Tolstoy, unconsciously used the phrases of Tolstoy himself. "Rightly or wrongly," he said, "for our chastisement perhaps, we have received from heaven that splendid and essential evil : thought. . . . To throw down this cross is an impious revolt." (*Le Roman russe*, 1886.) Now Tolstoy wrote to his aunt, the Countess A. A. Tolstoy, in 1883 : "Each of us must bear his cross. . . . Mine is the travail of the idea ; evil, full of pride and seductiveness." (*Letters.*)

there was a great risk that their art would be the first prey of the conflagration. They professed to believe that the whole art of literature was menaced; that the Russian, like Prospero, was burying for ever his magic ring with its power of creative illusion.

Nothing was further from the truth; and I hope to show that so far from ruining his art Tolstoy was awakening forces which had lain fallow, and that his religious faith, instead of killing his artistic genius, regenerated it completely.

XIII

SCIENCE
AND
ART

CHAPTER XIII

SCIENCE AND ART

IT is a singular fact that in speaking of Tolstoy's ideas concerning science and art, the most important of the books in which these ideas are expressed—namely, *What shall we do ?* (1884–86) —is commonly ignored. There, for the first time, Tolstoy fights the battle between art and science; and none of the following conflicts was to surpass the violence of their first encounter. It is a matter for surprise that no one, during the assaults which have been recently delivered in France upon the vanity of science and the intellectuals, has thought of referring to these pages. They constitute the most terrible attack ever penned against " the eunuchs of science " and " the corsairs of art " ; against those intellectual castes which, having destroyed the old ruling castes of the Church, the State, and the Army, have installed themselves in their place, and, without being able or willing to perform any service of use to humanity, lay claim to a blind admiration and service, proclaiming as dogmas an impudent faith in science for the sake of science and in art for the sake of art—the lying mask which they seek to make their justification and the apology for their monstrous egoism and their emptiness.

" Never make me say," continues Tolstoy, " that I deny art or science. Not only do I not deny them ; it is in their name that I seek to drive the thieves from the temple."

"Science and art are as necessary as bread and water; even more necessary. . . . The true science is that of the true welfare of all human beings. The true art is the expression of the knowledge of the true welfare of all men."

And he praises those who, " since men have existed, have with the harp or the cymbal, by images or by words, expressed their struggle against duplicity, their sufferings in that struggle, their hope in the triumph of good, their despair at the triumph of evil, and the enthusiasm of their prophetic vision of the future."

He then draws the character of the perfect artist, in a page burning with mystical and melancholy earnestness :

" The activity of science and art is only fruitful when it arrogates no right to itself and considers only its duties. It is only because that activity is such as it is, because its essence is sacrifice, that humanity honours it. The men who are called to serve others by spiritual work always suffer in the accomplishment of that task; for the spiritual world is brought to birth only in suffering and torture. Sacrifice and suffering ; such is the fate of the

thinker and the artist, for his fate is the good of
men. Men are unhappy ; they suffer ; they die ;
there is no time for him to stroll about, to amuse
himself. The thinker or the artist never strays upon
Olympian heights, as we are accustomed to think ;
he is always in a state of conflict, always in a
state of emotion. He must decide and must say
what will further the welfare of men, what will
deliver them from suffering; and he has not decided
it, he has not said it ; and to-morrow it will perhaps be too late, and he will die. . . . The man
who is trained in an establishment in which artists
and scientists are formed (to tell the truth, such
places make destroyers of art and of science) ; the
man who receives diplomas and a pension—he will
not be an artist or a thinker ; but he who would
be happy not to think, not to express what is implanted in his mind, yet cannot refrain from thought
and self-expression : for he is carried along by two
invisible forces : his inner need and his love of
men. There are no artists who are fat, lovers of
life, and satisfied with themselves." [1]

This splendid page, which throws a tragic light
upon the genius of Tolstoy, was written under the
immediate stress of the suffering caused him by
the poverty of Moscow, and under the conviction
that science and art were the accomplices of the
entire modern system of social inequality and
hypocritical brutality. This conviction he was
never to lose. But the impression of his first
encounter with the misery of the world slowly

[1] *What shall we do ?* p. 378–9.

faded, and became less poignant ; the wound healed,[1] and in none of his subsequent books do we recover the tremor of pain and of vengeful anger which vibrates in this; nowhere do we find this sublime profession of the faith of the artist who creates with his life-blood, this exaltation of the sacrifice and suffering " which are the lot of the thinker "; this disdain for Olympian art. Those of his later works which deal with the criticism of art will be found to treat the question from a standpoint at once more literary and less mystical ; the problem of art is detached from the background of that human wretchedness of which Tolstoy could not think without losing his self-control, as on the night of his visit to the night-shelter, when upon returning home he sobbed and cried aloud in desperation.

I do not mean to suggest that these didactic works are ever frigid. It is impossible for Tolstoy to be frigid. Until the end of his life he is the man who writes to Fet :

" If he does not love his personages, even the least of them, then he must insult them in such a way as to make the heavens fall, or must mock at them until he splits his sides." [2]

[1] In time he even came to justify suffering—not only personal suffering, but the sufferings of others. " For the assuagement of the sufferings of others is the essence of the rational life. How then should the object of labour be an object of suffering for the labourer ? It is as though the labourer were to say that an untilled field is a grief to him." (*Life*, chap. xxxiv.–xxxv.)

[2] February 23, 1860. *Further Letters*, pp. 19–20. It was for this reason that the " melancholy and dyspeptic " art of Tourgenev displeased him.

He does not forget to do so, in his writings on art. The negative portion of this statement—brimming over with insults and sarcasms—is so vigorously expressed that it is the only part which has struck the artist. This method has so violently wounded the superstitions and susceptibilities of the brotherhood that they inevitably see, in the enemy of their own art, the enemy of all art whatsoever. But Tolstoy's criticism is never devoid of the reconstructive element. He never destroys for the sake of destruction, but only to rebuild. In his modesty he does not even profess to build anything new; he merely defends Art, which was and ever shall be, from the false artists who exploit it and dishonour it.

"True science and true art have always existed and will always exist; it is impossible and useless to attack them," he wrote to me in 1887, in a letter which anticipated by more than ten years his famous criticism of art (*What is Art?*).[1] "All the evil of the day comes from the fact that so-called civilised people, together with the scientists and artists, form a privileged caste, like so many priests; and this caste has all the faults of all castes. It degrades and lowers the principle in virtue of which it was organised. What we in our world call the sciences and the arts is merely a gigantic *humbug*, a gross superstition into which we com-

---

[1] This letter (October 4, 1887) has been printed in the *Cahiers de la Quinzaine*, 1902, and in the *Further Letters* (*Correspondance inédite*), 1907. *What is Art?* appeared in 1897–98; but Tolstoy had been pondering the matter for more than fourteen years.

monly fall as soon as we free ourselves from the old superstition of the Church. To keep safely to the road we ought to follow we must begin at the beginning—we must raise the cowl which keeps us warm but obscures our sight. The temptation is great. We are born or we clamber upon the rungs of the ladder; and we find among the privileged the priests of civilisation, of *Kultur*, as the Germans have it. Like the Brahmin or Catholic priests, we must have a great deal of sincerity and a great love of the truth before we cast doubts upon the principles which assure us of our advantageous position. But a serious man who ponders the riddle of life cannot hesitate. To begin to see clearly he must free himself from his superstitions, however profitable they may be to him. This is a condition *sine quâ non*. . . . To have no superstition. To force oneself into the attitude of a child or a Descartes."

This superstition of modern art, in which the interested castes believe, "this gigantic humbug," is denounced in Tolstoy's *What is Art?* With a somewhat ungentle zest he holds it up to ridicule, and exposes its hypocrisy, its poverty, and its fundamental corruption. He makes a clean sweep of everything. He brings to this work of demolition the joy of a child breaking his toys. The whole of this critical portion is often full of humour, but sometimes of injustice: it is warfare. Tolstoy used all weapons that came to his hand, and struck at hazard, without noticing whom he struck. Often enough it happened—as in all battles—that he wounded those whom it should have been his duty to defend : Ibsen or Beethoven. This was the result of his enthusiasm, which left him no time to reflect before acting ; of his passion, which often blinded him to the weakness of his reasons, and— let us say it—it was also the result of his incomplete artistic culture.

Setting aside his literary studies, what could he well know of contemporary art ? When was he able to study painting, and what could he have heard of European music, this country gentleman who had passed three-fourths of his life in his Muscovite village, and who had not visited Europe since 1860 ; and what did he see when he was upon his travels, except the schools, which were all that interested him ? He speaks of paintings from hearsay, citing pell-mell among the decadents such painters as Puvis de Chavannes, Manet, Monet, Böcklin, Stuck, and Klinger ; confidently admiring Jules Breton and Lhermitte on account of their excellent sentiments ; despising Michelangelo, and among the painters of the soul never once naming Rembrandt. In music he felt his way better,[1] but knew hardly anything of it ; he could not get beyond the impressions of his childhood, swore by those who were already classics about 1840, and had not become familiar with any later composers (excepting Tchaikowsky, whose music made him weep) ; he throws Brahms and Richard Strauss into the bottom of the same bag, teaches Beethoven his

[1] I shall return to this matter when speaking of the *Kreutzer Sonata.*

business,[1] and, in order to judge Wagner, he thought it was sufficient to attend a single representation of *Siegfried*, at which he arrived after the rise of the curtain, while he left in the middle of the second act.[2] In the matter of literature he is, it goes without saying, rather better informed. But by what curious aberration did he evade the criticism of the Russian writers whom he knew so well, while he laid down the law to foreign poets, whose temperament was as far as possible removed from his own, and whose leaves he merely turned with contemptuous negligence ![3]

His intrepid assurance increased with age. It finally impelled him to write a book for the purpose of proving that Shakespeare " was not an artist."

" He may have been—no matter what : but he was not an artist." [4]

---

[1] His intolerance became aggravated after 1886. In *What shall we do?* he did not as yet dare to lay hands on Beethoven or on Shakespeare. Moreover, he reproached contemporary artists for daring to invoke their names. "The activity of a Galileo, a Shakespeare, a Beethoven has nothing in common with that of a Tyndall, a Victor Hugo, or a Wagner ; just as the Holy Father would deny all relationship with the Orthodox popes." (*What shall we do?*)

[2] For that matter, he wished to leave before the end of the first act. " For me the question was settled. I had no more doubt. There was nothing to be expected of an author capable of imagining scenes like these. One could affirm beforehand that he could never write anything that was not evil."

[3] In order to make a selection from the French poets of the new schools he conceived the admirable idea of " copying, in each volume, the verses printed on page 28 ! "

[4] *Shakespeare*, 1903. The book was written on the occasion of an article by Ernest Crosby upon *Shakespeare and the Working Classes.*

His certitude is admirable.   Tolstoy does not
doubt.   He does not discuss.   The truth is his.
He will tell you :

"The Ninth Symphony is a work which causes
social disunion."

Again :

"With the exception of the celebrated air for the
violin by Bach, the Nocturne in E flat by Chopin,
and a dozen pieces, not even entire, chosen from
among the works of Hadyn, Mozart, Weber,
Beethoven, and Chopin, . . . all the rest may be
rejected and treated with contempt, as examples of
an art which causes social disunion."

Again :

"I am going to prove that Shakespeare cannot
be ranked even as a writer of the fourth order.
And as a character-painter he is nowhere."

That the rest of humanity is of a different opinion
is no reason for hesitating :. on the contrary.

"My opinion," he proudly says, "is entirely
different from the established opinion concerning
Shakespeare throughout Europe."

Obsessed by his hatred of lies, he scents untruth
everywhere ; and the more widely an idea is
received, the more prickly he becomes in his
treatment of it; he refuses it, suspecting in it, as
he says with reference to the fame of Shakespeare,
"one of those epidemic influences to which men
have always been subject.   Such were the Crusades
in the Middle Ages, the belief in witchcraft, the
search for the philosopher's stone, and the passion
for tulips.   Men see the folly of these influences

only when they have won free from them. With
the development of the press these epidemics have
become particularly notable." And he gives as
an example the most recent of these contagious
diseases, the Dreyfus Affair, of which he, the enemy
of all injustice, the defender of all the oppressed,
speaks with disdainful indifference; [1] a striking
example of the excesses into which he is drawn by
his suspicion of untruth and that instinctive hatred
of "moral epidemics" of which he admits himself
the victim, and which he is unable to master. It is
the reverse side of a virtue, this inconceivable
blindness of the seer, the reader of souls, the
evoker of passionate forces, which leads him to
refer to *King Lear* as "an inept piece of work,"
and to the proud Cordelia as a "characterless
creature." [2]

[1] "Here was one of those incidents which often occur,
without attracting the attention of any one, and without
interesting—I do not say the world—but even the French
military world." And further on: "It was not until some
years had passed that men awoke from their hypnosis, and
understood that they could not possibly know whether Dreyfus
were guilty or not, and that each of them had other interests
more important and more immediate than the Affaire
Dreyfus." (*Shakespeare.*)

[2] "*King Lear* is a very poor drama, very carelessly constructed, which can inspire nothing but weariness and
disgust."—*Othello*, for which Tolstoy evinces a certain
sympathy, doubtless because the work is in harmony with
his ideas of that time concerning marriage and jealousy,
"while the least wretched of Shakespeare's plays, is only a
tissue of emphatic words." Hamlet has no character at all:
"he is the author's phonograph, who repeats all his ideas
in a string." As for *The Tempest, Cymbeline, Troilus and*

Observe that he sees very clearly certain of Shakespeare's actual defects—faults that we have not the sincerity to admit : the artificial quality of the poetic diction, which is uniformly attributed to all his characters ; and the rhetoric of passion, of heroism, and even of simplicity. I can perfectly well understand that a Tolstoy, who was the least literary of writers, should have been lacking in sympathy for the art of one who was the most genial of men of letters. But why waste time in speaking of that which he cannot understand ? What is the worth of judgments upon a world which is closed to the judge ?

Nothing, if we seek in these judgments the passport to these unfamiliar worlds. Inestimably great, if we seek in them the key to Tolstoy's art. We do not ask of a creative genius the impartiality of the critic. When a Wagner or a Tolstoy speaks of

Cressida, &c., Tolstoy only mentions them on account of their " ineptitude."

The only character of Shakespeare's whom he finds natural is Falstaff, " precisely because here the tongue of Shakespeare, full of frigid pleasantries and inept puns, is in harmony with the false, vain, debauched character of this repulsive drunkard."

Tolstoy had not always been of this opinion. He read Shakespeare with pleasure between 1860 and 1870, especially at the time when he contemplated writing a historical play about the figure of Peter the Great. In his notes for 1869 we find that he even takes *Hamlet* as his model and his guide. Having mentioned his completed works, and comparing *War and Peace* to the Homeric ideal, he adds :

" HAMLET and my future works ; the poetry of the romance-writer in the depicting of character."

Beethoven or of Shakespeare, he is speaking in reality not of Beethoven or of Shakespeare, but of himself ; he is revealing his own ideals. They do not even try to put us off the scent. Tolstoy, in criticising Shakespeare, does not attempt to make himself "objective." More : he reproaches Shakespeare for his objective art. The painter of *War and Peace*, the master of impersonal art, cannot sufficiently deride those German critics who, following the lead of Goethe, "invent Shakespeare," and are responsible for "the theory that art ought to be objective, that is to say, ought to represent human beings without any reference to moral values— which is the negation of the religious object of art."

It is thus from the pinnacle of a creed that Tolstoy pronounces his artistic judgments. We must not look for any personal after-thoughts in his criticisms. We shall find no trace of such a thing ; he is as pitiless to his own works as to those of others.[1] What, then, does he really intend ? What is the artistic significance of the religious ideal which he proposes ?

This ideal is magnificent. The term "religious art" is apt to mislead one as to the breadth of the conception. Far from narrowing the province of art, Tolstoy enlarges it. Art, he says, is everywhere.

"Art creeps into our whole life ; what we term

[1] He classes his own "works of imagination" in the category of "harmful art." (*What is Art ?*) From this condemnation he does not except his own plays, "devoid of that religious conception which must form the basis of the drama of the future."

art, namely, theatres, concerts, books, exhibitions, is only an infinitesimal portion of art. Our life is full of artistic manifestations of every kind, from the games of children to the offices of religion. Art and speech are the two organs of human progress. One affords the communion of hearts, the other the communion of thoughts. If either of the two is perverted, then society is sick. The art of to-day is perverted."

Since the Renascence it has no longer been possible to speak of the art of the Christian nations. Class has separated itself from class. The rich, the privileged, have attempted to claim the monopoly of art; and they have made their pleasure the criterion of beauty. Art has become impoverished as it has grown remoter from the poor.

"The category of the emotions experienced by those who do not work in order to live is far more limited than the emotions of those who labour. The sentiments of our modern society may be reduced to three : pride, sensuality, and weariness of life. These three sentiments and their ramifications constitute almost entirely the subject of the art of the wealthy."

It infects the world, perverts the people, propagates sexual depravity, and has become the worst obstacle to the realisation of human happiness. It is also devoid of real beauty, unnatural and insincere ; an affected, fabricated, cerebral art.

In the face of this lie of the æsthetics, this pastime of the rich, let us raise the banner of the living, human art : the art which unites the men of all classes and all nations. The past offers us glorious examples of such art.

"The majority of mankind has always understood and loved that which we consider the highest art : the epic of Genesis, the parables of the Gospel, the legends, tales, and songs of the people."

The greatest art is that which expresses the religious conscience of the period. By this Tolstoy does not mean the teaching of the Church. "Every society has a religious conception of life ; it is the ideal of the greatest happiness towards which that society tends." All are to a certain extent aware of this tendency ; a few pioneers express it clearly.

"A religious conscience always exists. IT IS THE BED IN WHICH THE RIVER FLOWS."

The religious consciousness of our epoch is the aspiration toward happiness as realised by the fraternity of mankind. There is no true art but that which strives for this union. The highest art is that which accomplishes it directly by the power of love ; but there is another art which participates in the same task, by attacking, with the weapons of scorn and indignation, all that opposes this fraternity. Such are the novels of Dickens and Dostoyevsky, Victor Hugo's *Les Misérables*, and the paintings of Millet. But even though it fail to attain these heights, all art which represents daily life with sympathy and truth brings men nearer together. Such is *Don Quixote:* such are the plays of Molière. It is true that such art as the latter is continually sinning by its too minute realism and by the poverty of its subjects " when compared with ancient models, such as the sublime history of Joseph." The excessive minuteness of detail is detrimental to such works, which for that reason cannot become universal.

"Modern works of art are spoiled by a realism which might more justly be called the provincialism of art."

Thus Tolstoy unhesitatingly condemns the principle of his own genius. What does it signify to him that he should sacrifice himself to the future—and that nothing of his work should remain ?

"The art of the future will not be a development of the art of the present: it will be founded upon other bases. It will no longer be the property of a caste. Art is not a trade or profession : it is the expression of real feelings. Now the artist can only experience real feelings when he refrains from isolating himself ; when he lives the life natural to man. For this reason the man who is sheltered from life is in the worst possible conditions for creative work."

In the future "artists will all be endowed." Artistic activity will be made accessible to all "by the introduction into the elementary schools of instruction in music and painting, which will be taught to the child simultaneously with the first principles of grammar." For the rest, art will no longer call for a complicated technique, as at present ; it will move in the direction of simplicity, clearness, and conciseness, which are the marks of sane and classic art, and of Homeric art.[1] How pleasant it will be to translate universal sentiments into the pure lives of this art of the future ! To write a tale or a song, to design a picture for millions of beings, is a matter of much greater importance—and of much greater difficulty—than writing a novel or a symphony. It is an immense and almost virgin province. Thanks to such works men will learn to appreciate the happiness of brotherly union.

"Art must suppress violence, and only art can do so. Its mission is to bring about the Kingdom of God, that is to say, of Love."[2]

Which of us would not endorse these generous words ? And who can fail to see that Tolstoy's conception is fundamentally fruitful and vital, in spite of its Utopianism and a touch of puerility ? It is true that our art as a whole is only the

[1] As early as 1873 Tolstoy had written : "Think what you will, but in such a fashion that every word may be understood by every one. One cannot write anything bad in a perfectly clear and simple language. What is immoral will appear so false if clearly expressed that it will assuredly be deleted. If a writer seriously wishes to speak to the people, he has only to force himself to be comprehensible. When not a word arrests the reader's attention the work is good. If he cannot relate what he has read the work is worthless."

[2] This ideal of brotherhood and union among men is by no means, to Tolstoy's mind, the limit of human activity ; his insatiable mind conceives an unknown ideal, above and beyond that of love :

"Science will perhaps one day offer as the basis of art a much higher ideal, and art will realise it."

expression of a caste, which is itself subdivided not only by the fact of nationality, but in each country also into narrow and hostile clans. There is not a single artist in Europe who realises in his own personality the union of parties and of races. The most universal mind of our time was that of Tolstoy himself. In him men of all nations and all classes have attained fraternity; and those who have tasted the virile joy of this capacious love can no longer be satisfied by the shreds and fragments of the vast human soul which are offered by the art of the European cliques.

XIV

THEORIES
OF ART:
MUSIC

CHAPTER XIV

THEORIES OF ART : MUSIC

THE finest theory finds its value only in the works by which it is exemplified. With Tolstoy theory and creation are always hand in hand, like faith and action. While he was elaborating his critique of art he was producing types of the new art of which he spoke : of two forms of art, one higher and one less exalted, but both "religious" in the most human sense. In one he sought the union of men through love; in the other he waged war upon the world, the enemy of love. It was during this period that he wrote those masterpieces : *The Death of Ivan Ilyitch* (1884–86), the *Popular Tales and Stories* (1881–1886), *The Power of Darkness* (1886), the *Kreutzer Sonata* (1889), and *Master and Servant* (1895).[1]

[1] To these years was attributed, in respect of the date of publication, and perhaps of completion, a work which was really written during the happy period of betrothal and the first years of marriage : the beautiful story of a horse, *Kholstomier* (1861–86). Tolstoy speaks of it in 1883 in a letter to Fet (*Further Correspondence*). The art of the commencement, with its fine landscapes, its penetrating psychological sympathy, its humour, and its youth, has

At the height and end of this artistic period, like a cathedral with two spires, the one symbolising eternal love and the other the hatred of the world, stands *Resurrection* (1899).

All these works are distinguished from their predecessors by new artistic qualities. Tolstoy's ideas had suffered a change, not alone in respect of the object of art, but also in respect of its form. In reading *What is Art?* or *Shakespeare* we are struck by the principles of art which Tolstoy has enounced in these two books; for these principles are for the most part in contradiction to the greatest of his previous works. "Clearness, simplicity, conciseness," we read in *What is Art?* Material effects are despised; minute realism is condemned; and in *Shakespeare* the classic ideal of perfection and proportion is upheld. "Without the feeling of balance no artists could exist." And although in his new work the unregenerate man, with his genius for analysis and his native savagery, is not entirely effaced, some aspects of the latter quality being even emphasised, his art is profoundly modified in some respects : the design is clearer, more vigorously accented ; the minds of his characters are epitomised, foreshortened ; the interior drama is intensified, gathered upon itself like a beast of prey about

much in common with the art of Tolstoy's maturity (*Family Happiness, War and Peace*). The *macabre* quality of the end, and the last pages comparing the body of the old horse with that of his master, are full of a realistic brutality characteristic of the years after 1880.

to spring; the emotion has a quality of universality ; and is freed of all transitory details of local
realism ; and finally the diction is rich in
illustrations, racy, and smacking of the soil.

His love of the people had long led him to appreciate the beauty of the popular idiom. As a child
he had been soothed by the tales of mendicant
story-tellers. As a grown man and a famous writer,
he experienced an artistic delight in chatting with
his peasants.

"These men," he said in later years to M. Paul
Boyer,[1] "are masters. Of old, when I used to talk
with them, or with the wanderers who, wallet on
shoulder, pass through our countryside, I used care-
fully to note such of their expressions as I heard
for the first time ; expressions often forgotten by our
modern literary dialect, but always good old
Russian currency, ringing sound. . . . Yes, the
genius of the language lives in these men."

He must have been the more sensitive to such
elements of the language in that his mind was not
encumbered with literature.[2] Through living far
from any city, in the midst of peasants, he came
to think a little in the manner of the people. He
had the slow dialectic, the common sense which
reasons slowly and painfully, step by step, with

[1] *Le Temps*, August 29, 1901.

[2] "As for style," his friend Droujinin told him in 1856,
"You are extremely illiterate ; sometimes like an innovator
and a great poet ; sometimes like an officer writing to a comrade. All that you write with real pleasure is admirable.
The moment you become indifferent your style becomes
involved and is horrible." (*Vie et Œuvre.*)

sudden disconcerting leaps, the mania for repeating
any idea when he was once convinced, of repeating
it unwearingly and indefinitely, and in the same
words.[1]

But these were faults rather than qualities. It
was many years before he became aware of the
latent genius of the popular tongue ; the raciness
of its images, its poetic crudity, its wealth of
legendary wisdom. Even at the time of writing
War and Peace he was already subject to its influence. In March, 1872, he wrote to Strakov :

" I have altered the method of my diction and my
writing. The language of the people has sounds to
express all that the poet can say, and it is very dear
to me. It is the best poetic regulator. If you try
to say anything superfluous, too emphatic, or false,
the language will not suffer it. Whereas our literary
tongue has no skeleton, you may pull it about in
every direction, and the result is always something
resembling literature."

To the people he owed not only models of style ;
he owed them many of his inpirations. In 1877 a
teller of *bylines* came to Yasnaya Polyana, and
Tolstoy took notes of several of his stories. Of the
number was the legend *By what do Men live ?* and
The Three Old Men, which became, as we know, two
of the finest of the *Popular Tales and Legends* which
Tolstoy published a few years later.[2]

---

[1] *Vie et Œuvre.*—During the summer of 1879 Tolstoy lived
on terms of great intimacy with the peasants.

[2] In the notes of his readings, between 1860 and 1870,
Tolstoy wrote : " The *bylines*—very greatly impressed."

This is a work unique in modern art. It is higher than art : for who, in reading it, thinks of literature ? The spirit of the Gospel and the pure love of the brotherhood of man are combined with the smiling geniality of the wisdom of the people. It is full of simplicity, limpidity, and ineffable goodness of heart ; and that supernatural radiance which from time to time—so naturally and inevitably—bathes the whole picture ; surrounding the old Elias [1] like a halo, or hovering in the cabin of the cobbler Michael ; he who, through his skylight on the ground-level, sees the feet of people passing, and whom the Lord visits in the guise of the poor whom the good cobbler has succoured.[2] Sometimes in these tales the parables of the Gospel are mingled with a vague perfume of Oriental legends, of those *Thousand and One Nights* which Tolstoy had loved since childhood.[3] Sometimes, again, the fantastic light takes on a sinister aspect, lending the tale a terrifying majesty. Such is *Pakhom the Peasant*,[4] the tale of the man who kills himself in acquiring a great surface of and—all the land which he can encircle by walking for a whole day—and who dies on completing his journey.

" On the hill the *starschina*, sitting on the ground, watched him as he ran ; and he cackled, holding his stomach with both hands. And Pakhom fell.

---

[1] *The Two Old Men* (1885).

[2] *Where Love is, there God is also* (1885).

[3] *By what do Men live ?* (1881) ; *The Three Old Men* (1884) ; *The Godchild* (1886).

[4] This tale bears the sub-title, *Does a Man need much Soil ?* (1886).

" ' Ah !   Well done, my merry fellow !   You have won a mighty lot of land ! '

" The *starschina* rose, and threw a mattock to Pakhom's servant.

" ' There he is : bury him.'

" The servant was alone. He dug a ditch for Pakhom, just as long as from his feet to his head : two yards, and he buried him."

Nearly all these tales conceal, beneath their poetic envelope, the same evangelical moral of renunciation and pardon.

" Do not avenge thyself upon whosoever shall offend thee.[1]

" Do not resist whosoever shall do thee evil.[2]

" Vengeance is Mine, saith the Lord."[3]

And everywhere, and as the conclusion of all, is love.

Tolstoy, who wished to found an art for all men, achieved universality at the first stroke.   Throughout the world his work has met with a success which can never fail, for it is purged of all the perishable elements of art, and nothing is left but the eternal.

The Power oj Darkness does not rise to this august simplicity of heart : it does not pretend to do so.   It is the reverse side of the picture.   On the one hand is the dream of divine love ; on the other, the ghastly reality.   We may judge, in reading this

---

[1] *The Fire that flames does not go out* (1885).
[2] *The Wax Taper* (1885) ; *The Story of Ivan the Idiot.*
[3] *The Godson* (1886).

play, whether Tolstoy's faith and his love of the
people ever caused him to idealise the people or
betray the truth.

Tolstoy, so awkward in most of his dramatic
essays,[1] has here attained to mastery. The
characters and the action, are handled with ease ;
the coxcomb Nikita, the sensual, headstrong passion
of Anissia, the cynical good-humour of the old
woman, Matrena, who gloats maternally over the
adultery of her son, and the sanctity of the old
stammering Hakim—God inhabiting a ridiculous
body. Then comes the fall of Nikita, weak and
without real evil, but fettered by his sin ; falling to
the depths of crime in spite of his efforts to check
himself on the dreadful declivity ; but his mother
and his wife drag him downward. . . .

"The peasants aren't worth much. . . . But the
babas ! The women ! They are wild animals . . .
they are afraid of nothing ! . . . Sisters, there are

---

[1] The love of the theatre came to him somewhat late in life.
It was a discovery of his, and he made this discovery during
the winter of 1869–70. According to his custom, he was at
once afire with enthusiasm.

"All this winter I have busied myself exclusively with the
drama ; and, as always happens to men who have never, up to
the age of forty, thought about such or such a subject, when
they suddenly turn their attention to this neglected subject, it
seems to them that they perceive a number of new and
wonderful things. . . . I have read Shakespeare, Goethe,
Pushkin, Gogol, and Molière. . . . I want to read Sophocles
and Euripides. . . . I have kept my bed a long time, being
unwell—and when I am unwell a host of comic or dramatic
characters begin to struggle for life within me . . . and they
do it with much success."—Letters to Fet, February 17–21,
1870 (*Further Letters*).

millions of you, all Russians, and you are all as blind as moles. You know nothing, you know nothing ! . . . The moujik at least may manage to learn something—in the drink-shop, or who knows where ?—in prison, or in the barracks; but the *baba*—what can she know ? She has seen nothing, heard nothing. As she has grown up, so she will die. . . . They are like little blind puppies who go running here and there and ramming their heads against all sorts of filth. . . . They only know their silly songs : ' Ho—o—o ! Ho—o—o !' What does it mean ? Ho—o—o ? They don't know !" [1]

Then comes the terrible scene of the murder of the new-born child. Nikita does not want to kill it. Anissia, who has murdered her husband for him, and whose nerves have ever since been tortured by her crime, becomes ferocious, maddened, and threatens to give him up. She cries :

"At least I shan't be alone any longer ! He'll be a murderer too ! Let him know what it's like !"

Nikita crushes the child between two boards. In the midst of his crime he flies, terrified ; he threatens to kill Anissia and his mother ; he sobs, he prays :—

"Little mother, I can't go on !" He thinks he hears the mangled baby crying.

"Where shall I go to be safe ?"

It is Shakespearean. Less violent, but still more poignant, is the dialogue of the little girl and the old servant-woman, who, alone in the house, at

[1] A variant of Act iv.

night, hear and guess at the crime which is being enacted off the stage.

The end is voluntary expiation. Nikita, accompanied by his father, the old Hakim, enters barefooted, in the midst of a wedding. He kneels, asks pardon of all, and accuses himself of every crime. Old Hakim encourages him, looks upon him with a smile of ecstatic suffering.

"God! Oh, look at him, God!"

The drama gains quite a special artistic flavour by the use of the peasant dialect.

"I ransacked my notebooks in order to write *The Power of Darkness*," Tolstoy told M. Paul Boyer.

The unexpected images, flowing from the lyrical yet humorous soul of the Russian people, have a swing and a vigour about them beside which images of the more literary quality seem tame and colourless. Tolstoy revelled in them; we feel, in reading the play, that the artist while writing it amused himself by noting these expressions, these turns of thought; the comic side of them by no means escapes him,[1] even while the apostle is mourning amidst the dark places of the human soul.

While he was studying the people, and sending into their darkness a ray of light from his station above them, he was also devoting two tragic romances to the still darker night of the middle

---

[1] The creation of this heart-breaking drama must have been a strain. He writes to Teneromo: "I am well and happy. I have been working all this time at my play. It is finished." (January, 1887. *Further Letters*.)

classes and the wealthy. At this period the dramatic form was predominant over his ideas of art. The *Death of Ivan Ilyitch* and *The Kreutzer Sonata* are both true dramas of the inner soul, of the soul turned upon itself and concentrated upon itself, and in *The Kreutzer Sonata* it is the hero of the drama himself who unfolds it by narration.

The Death of Ivan Ilyitch (1884–86) has impressed the French public as few Russian works have done. At the beginning of this study I mentioned that I had witnessed the sensation caused by this book among the middle-class readers in the French provinces, a class apparently indifferent to literature and art. I think the explanation lies in the fact that the book represents, with a painful realism, a type of the average, mediocre man; a conscientious functionary, without religion, without ideals, almost without thought; the man who is absorbed in his duties, in his mechanical life, until the hour of his death, when he sees with terror that he has not lived. Ivan Ilyitch is the representative type of the European *bourgeoisie* of 1880 which reads Zola, goes to hear Bernhardt, and, without holding any faith, is not even irreligious; for it does not take the trouble either to believe or to disbelieve; it simply never thinks of such matters.

In the violence of its attacks, alternately bitter and almost comic, upon the world in general, and marriage in particular, the *Death of Ivan Ilyitch* was the first of a new series of works; it was the forerunner of the still more morose and unworldly *Kreutzer Sonata* and *Resurrection*. There is a lamentable yet laughable emptiness in this life (as there is in thousands and thousands of lives), with its grotesque ambitions, its wretched gratification of vanity, "always better than spending the evening opposite one's wife"; with its weariness and hatred of the official career; its privileges, and the embitterment which they cause; and its one real pleasure: whist. This ridiculous life is lost for a cause yet more ridiculous—a fall from a ladder, one day when Ivan wished to hang a curtain over the drawing-room window. The lie of life. The lie of sickness. The lie of the well-to-do doctor, who thinks only of himself. The lie of the family, whom illness disgusts. The lie of the wife, who professes devotion, and calculates how she will live when her husband is dead. The universal lie, against which is set only the truth of a compassionate servant, who does not try to conceal his condition from the dying man, and helps him out of brotherly kindness. Ivan Ilyitch, "full of an infinite pity for himself," weeps over his loneliness and the egoism of men ; he suffers horribly, until the day on which he perceives that his past life has been a lie, and that he can repair that lie. Immediately all becomes clear—an hour before his death. He no longer thinks of himself; he thinks of his family; he pities them; he *must* die and rid them of himself.

"Where are you, Pain? Here. . . . Well, you have only to persist.—And Death, where is Death? He did not find it. In place of Death he saw only a ray of light. 'It is over,' said some one.—He heard these words and repeated them to himself. 'Death no longer exists,' he told himself."

In *The Kreutzer Sonata* there is not even this "ray of light." It is a ferocious piece of work ; Tolstoy lashes out at society like a wounded beast avenging itself for what it has suffered. We must not forget that the story is the confession of a human brute, who has taken life, and who is poisoned by the virus of jealousy. Tolstoy hides himself behind his leading character. We certainly find his own ideas, though heightened in tone, in these furious invectives against hypocrisy in general ; the hypocrisy of the education of women, of love, of marriage— marriage, that "domestic prostitution" ; the hypocrisy of the world, of science, of physicians—those "sowers of crime." But the hero of the book impels the writer into an extraordinary brutality of expression, a violent rush of carnal images—all the excesses of a luxurious body—and, by reaction into all the fury of asceticism, the fear and hatred of the passions ; maledictions hurled in the face of life by a monk of the Middle Ages, consumed with sensuality. Having written the book Tolstoy himself was alarmed :

"I never foresaw at all," he said in the *Epilogue to the Kreutzer Sonata*," [1] that in writing this book a rigorous logic would bring me where I have arrived. My own conclusions terrified me at first, and I was tempted to reject them ; but it was impossible for

[1] A French translation of this Epilogue (*Postface*), by M. Halpérine-Kaminsky was published in the volume *Plaisirs vicieux*, under the title *Des relations entre les sexes*.

me to refuse to hear the voice of my reason and my conscience."

He found himself repeating, in calmer tones, the savage outcry of the murderer Posdnicheff against love and marriage.

" He who regards woman—above all his wife—with sensuality, already commits adultery with her."

" When the passions have disappeared, then humanity will no longer have a reason for being; it will have executed the Law ; the union of mankind will be accomplished."

He will prove, on the authority of the Gospel according to Matthew, that "the Christian ideal is not marriage ; that Christian marriage cannot exist ; that marriage, from the Christian point of view, is an element not of progress but of downfall; that love, with all that precedes and follows it, is an obstacle to the true human ideal." [1]

But he had never formulated these ideas clearly, even to himself, until they fell from the lips of Posdnicheff. As often happens with great creative artists, the work carried the writer with it; the artist outstripped the thinker ; a process by which

[1] Let us take notice that Tolstoy was never guilty of the simplicity of believing that the ideal of celibacy and absolute chastity was capable of realisation by humanity as we know it. But according to him an ideal is incapable of realisation by its very definition : it is an appeal to the heroic energies of the soul.

" The conception of the Christian ideal, which is the union of all living creatures in brotherly love, is irreconcilable with the conduct of life, which demands a continual effort towards an ideal which is inaccessible, but does not expect that it will ever be attained."

art lost nothing. In the power of its effects, in passionate concentration, in the brutal vividness of its impressions, and in fullness and maturity of form, nothing Tolstoy has written equals the *Kreutzer Sonata.*

I have not explained the title. To be exact, it is erroneous; it gives a false idea of the book, in which music plays only an accessory part. Suppress the sonata, and all would be the same. Tolstoy made the mistake of confusing two matters, both of which he took deeply to heart : the depraving power of music, and the depraving power of love. The demon of music should have been dealt with in a separate volume ; the space which Tolstoy has accorded it in the work in question is insufficient to prove the danger which he wishes to denounce. I must emphasise this matter somewhat ; for I do not think the attitude of Tolstoy in respect of music has ever been fully understood.

He was far from disliking music. Only the things one loves are feared as Tolstoy feared the power of music. Remember what a place the memories of music hold in *Childhood,* and above all in *Family Happiness,* in which the whole cycle of love, from its springtide to its autumn, is unrolled to the phrases of the *Sonata quasi una fantasia* of Beethoven. Remember, too, the wonderful symphonies which Nekhludov [1] hears in fancy, and the little Petia, the night before his death.[2] Although

[1] At the end of *A Russian Proprietor.*

[2] *War and Peace.*—I do not mention *Albert* (1857), the story of a musician of genius ; the book is weak in the extreme.

Tolstoy had studied music very indifferently, it used to move him to tears, and at certain periods of his life he passionately abandoned himself to its influence. In 1858 he founded a Musical Society, which in later years became the Moscow Conservatoire.

"He was extremely fond of music," writes his brother-in-law, S. A. Bers. "He used to play the piano, and was fond of the classic masters. He would often sit down to the piano before beginning his work.[1] Probably he found inspiration in so doing. He always used to accompany my youngest sister, whose voice he loved. I have noticed that the sensations which the music evoked in him were accompanied by a slight pallor and an imperceptible grimace, which seemed expressive of fear."[2]

It was really fear that he felt; fear inspired by the stress of those unknown forces which shook him to the roots of his being. In the world of music he felt his moral will, his reason, and all the reality of life dissolve. Let us turn to the scene, in the first volume of *War and Peace*, in which Nikolas Rostoff, who has just lost heavily at cards, returns in a state of despair. He hears his sister Natasha singing. He forgets everything.

"He waited with a feverish impatience for the note which was about to follow, and for a moment the only thing in all the world was the melody in three-quarter-time: *Oh! mio crudele affetto!*

---

[1] The period spoken of is 1876–77.
[2] S. A. Bers, *Memories of Tolstoy*.

"'What an absurd existence ours is!' he thought. 'Unhappiness, money, hatred, honour—they are all nothing. . . . Here is the truth, the reality! . . . Natasha, my little dove! . . . Let us see if she is going to reach that B? . . . She has reached it, thank God!'

"And to emphasise the B he sung the third octave below it in accompaniment.

"'How splendid! I have sung it too,' he cried, and the vibration of that octave awoke in his soul all that was best and purest. Beside this superhuman sensation, what were his losses at play and his word of honour? . . . Follies! One could kill, steal, and yet be happy!"

Nikolas neither kills nor steals, and for him music is only a passing influence; but Natasha is on the point of losing her self-control. After an evening at the Opera, "in that strange world which is intoxicated and perverted by art, and a thousand leagues from the real world; a world in which good and evil, the extravagant and the reasonable, are mingled and confounded," she listened to a declaration from Anatol Kouraguin, who was madly in love with her, and she consented to elope with him.

The older Tolstoy grew, the more he feared music.[1] A man whose influence over him was

---

[1] But he never ceased to love it. One of the friends of his later years was a musician, Goldenreiser, who spent the summer of 1910 near Yasnaya. Almost every day he came to play to Tolstoy during the latter's last illness. (*Journal des Débats*, November 18, 1910.)

considerable—Auerbach, whom in 1860 he had met in Dresden—had doubtless a hand in fortifying his prejudices. "He spoke of music as of a *Pflichtloser Genuss* (a profligate amusement). According to him, it was an incentive to depravity." [1]

Among so many musicians, some of whose music is at least amoral, why, asks M. Camille Bellaigue,[2] should Tolstoy have chosen Beethoven, the purest, the chastest of all ?—Because he was the most powerful. Tolstoy had early loved his music, and he always loved it. His remotest memories of *Childhood* were connected with the *Sonata Pathétique;* and when Nekhludov in *Resurrection* heard the *andante* of the *Symphony in C Minor,* he could hardly restrain his tears : "he was filled with tenderness for himself and for those he loved." Yet we have seen with what animosity Tolstoy referred in his *What is Art?*[3] to the "unhealthy works of the deaf Beethoven"; and even in 1876 the fury with which "he delighted in demolishing Beethoven and in casting doubts upon his genius" had revolted Tchaikowsky and had diminished his admiration for Tolstoy. The *Kreutzer Sonata* enables us to plumb the depths of

---

[1] Letter of April 21, 1861.

[2] *Tolstoï et la musique* (*Le Gaulois,* January 4, 1911).

[3] Not only to the later works of Beethoven. Even in the case of those earlier works which he consented to regard as "artistic," Tolstoy complained of "their artificial form."—In a letter to Tchaikowsky he contrasts with Mozart and Haydn "the artificial manner of Beethoven, Schubert, and Berlioz, which produces calculated effects."

this passionate injustice. What does Tolstoy complain of in Beethoven? Of his power. He
reminds us of Goethe; listening to the *Symphony in C Minor*, he is overwhelmed by it, and
angrily turns upon the imperious master who
subjects him against his will.[1]

"This music," says Tolstoy, "transports me
immediately into the state of mind which was
the composer's when he wrote it. . . . Music
ought to be a State matter, as in China. We
ought not to let Tom, Dick, and Harry wield so
frightful a hypnotic power. . . . As for these things
(the first *Presto* of the Sonata) one ought only to
be allowed to play them under particular and
important circumstances. . . ."

Yet we see, after this revolt, how he surrenders
to the power of Beethoven, and how this power
is by his own admission a pure and ennobling
force. On hearing the piece in question, Posdnicheff
falls into an indefinable state of mind, which he
cannot analyse, but of which the consciousness
fills him with delight. "There is no longer room
for jealousy." The wife is not less transfigured.
She has, while she plays, "a majestic severity of
expression"; and "a faint smile, compassionate
and happy, after she has finished." What is there
perverse in all this? This: that the spirit is

---

[1] Instance the scene described by M. Paul Boyer:
"Tolstoy sat down to play Chopin. At the end of the
fourth Ballade, his eyes filled with tears. 'Ah, the animal!'
he cried. And suddenly he rose and went out." (*Le Temps*,
November 2, 1902.)

enslaved : that the unknown power of sound can do with him what it wills; destroy him, if it please.

This is true, but Tolstoy forgets one thing : the mediocrity and the lack of vitality in the majority of those who make or listen to music. Music cannot be dangerous to those who feel nothing. The spectacle of the Opera-house during a performance of *Salomé* is quite enough to assure us of the immunity of the public to the more perverse emotions evoked by the art of sounds. To be in danger one must be, like Tolstoy, abounding in life. The truth is that in spite of his injustice where Beethoven was concerned, Tolstoy felt his music more deeply than do the majority of those who now exalt him. He, at least, knew the frenzied passions, the savage violence, which mutter through the art of the " deaf old man," but of which the orchestras and the virtuosi of to-day are innocent. Beethoven would perhaps have preferred the hatred of Tolstoy to the enthusiasm of his admirers.

XV

"RESURRECTION"

CHAPTER XV

" RESURRECTION "

TEN years separated *Resurrection* from the *Kreutzer Sonata ;* [1] ten years which were more and more absorbed in moral propaganda. Ten years also separated the former book from the end for which this life hungered, famished as it was for the eternal. *Resurrection* is in a sense the artistic testament of the author. It dominates the end of his life as *War and Peace* crowned its maturity. It is the last peak, perhaps the highest—if not the most stupendous—

[1] *Master and Servant* (1895) is more or less of a transition between the gloomy novels which preceded it and *Resurrection ;* which is full of the light of the Divine charity. But it is akin to *The Death of Ivan Ilyitch* and the *Popular Tales* rather than to *Resurrection,* which only presents, towards the end of the book, the sublime transformation of a selfish and morally cowardly man under the stress of an impulse of sacrifice. The greater part of the book consists of the extremely realistic picture of a master without kindness and a servant full of resignation, who are surprised, by night, on the steppes, by a blizzard, in which they lose their way. The master, who at first tries to escape, deserting his companion, returns, and finding the latter half-frozen, throws himself upon him, covering him with his body, gives him of his warmth, and sacrifices himself by instinct ; he does not know

whose invisible summit is lost in the mists. Tolstoy is seventy years old. He contemplates the world, his life, his past mistakes, his faith, his righteous anger.

He sees them from a height. We find the same ideals as in his previous books ; the same warring upon hypocrisy ; but the spirit of the artist, as in *War and Peace*, soars above his subject. To the sombre irony, the mental tumult of the *Kreutzer Sonata* and *The Death of Ivan Ilyitch* he adds a religious serenity, a detachment from the world, which is faithfully reflected in himself. One is reminded, at times, of a Christian Goethe.

All the literary characteristics which we have noted in the works of his later period are to be found here, and of these especially the concentration of the narrative, which is even more striking in a long novel than in a short story. There is a wonderful unity about the book ; in which respect it differs widely from *War and Peace* and *Anna Karenin*. There are hardly any digressions of an episodic nature. A single train of action, tenaciously

why, but the tears fill his eyes ; it seems to him that he has become the man he is seeking to save—Nikita—and that his life is no longer in himself, but in Nikita. "Nikita is alive ; then I am still alive, myself." He has almost forgotten who he, Vassili, was. He thinks : "Vassili did not know what had to be done. But I, I know !" He hears the voice of Him whom he was awaiting (here his dream recalls one of the *Popular Tales*), of Him who, a little while ago, had commanded him to lie upon Nikita. He cries, quite happy : "Lord, I am coming !" and he feels that he is free ; that nothing is keeping him back any longer. He is dead.

followed, is worked out in every detail. There is the same vigorous portraiture, the same ease and fullness of handling, as in the *Kreutzer Sonata*. The observation is more than ever lucid, robust, pitilessly realistic, revealing the animal in the man —"the terrible persistence of the beast in man, more terrible when this animality is not openly obvious ; when it is concealed under a so-called poetical exterior." Witness the drawing-room conversations, which have for their object the mere satisfaction of a physical need : "the need of stimulating the digestion by moving the muscles of the tongue and gullet" ; the crude vision of humanity which spares no one ; neither the pretty Korchagina, "with her two false teeth, the salient bones of her elbows, and the largeness of her finger-nails," and her *décolletage*, which inspires in Nekhludov a feeling of "shame and disgust, disgust and shame" ; nor the herione, Maslova, nothing of whose degradation is hidden ; her look of premature age, her vicious, ignoble expression, her provocative smile, the odour of brandy that hangs about her, her red and swollen face. There is a brutality of naturalistic detail : as instance, the woman who converses while crouched over the commode. Youth and the poetic imagination have vanished ; except in the passages which deal with the memories of first love, whose music vibrates in the reader's mind with hypnotic intensity ; the night of the Holy Saturday, and the night of Passover ; the thaw, the white mist so thick "that at five paces from the house one saw nothing but a shadowy mass, whence glimmered the red light of a lamp " ; the crowing of the cocks in the night ; the sounds from the frozen river, where the ice cracks, snores, bubbles, and tinkles like a breaking glass ; and the young man who, from the night outside, looks through the window at the young girl who does not see him : seated near the table in the flickering light of the little lamp— Katusha, pensive, dreaming, and smiling at her dreams.

The lyrical powers of the writer are given but little play. His art has become more impersonal ; more alien to his own life. The world of criminals and revolutionaries, which he here describes, was unfamiliar to him ;[1] he enters it only by an effort of voluntary sympathy ; he even admits that before studying them at close quarters the revolutionaries inspired him with an unconquerable aversion. All the more admirable is his impeccable observation—a faultless mirror. What a wealth of types, of precise details ! How everything is *seen ;* baseness and virtue, without hardness, without weakness, but with a serene understanding and a brotherly pity. . . . The terrible picture of the women in the prison ! They are pitiless to one another ; but the artist is the merciful God ; he sees, in the heart of each, the distress that hides beneath humiliation, and the tearful eyes beneath

---

[1] While on the other hand he had mixed in all the various circles depicted in *War and Peace, Anna Karenin, The Cossacks,* and *Sebastopol ;* the *salons* of the nobles, the army, the life of the country estate. He had only to remember.

the mask of effrontery. The pure, faint light which little by little waxes within the vicious mind of Maslova, and at last illumines her with a sacrificial flame, has the touching beauty of one of those rays of sunshine which transfigure some humble scene painted by the brush of Rembrandt. There is no severity here, even for the warders and executioners. " Lord, forgive them, for they know not what they do !" . . . The worst of it is that often they do know what they do ; they feel all the pangs of remorse, yet they cannot do otherwise. There broods over the book the sense of the crushing and inevitable fatality which weighs upon those who suffer and those who cause that suffering : the director of the prison, full of natural kindness, as sick of his jailer's life as of the pianoforte exercises of the pale, sickly daughter with the dark circles beneath her eyes, who indefatigably murders a rhapsody of Liszt ; the Governor-General of the Siberian town, intelligent and kindly, who, in the hope of escaping the inevitable conflict between the good he wishes to do and the evil he is forced to do, has been steadily drinking since the age of thirty-five ; who is always sufficiently master of himself to keep up appearances, even when he is drunk. And among these people we find the ordinary affection for wife and children, although their calling renders them pitiless in respect of the rest of humanity.

The only character in this book who has no objective reality is Nekhludov himself ; and this is so because Tolstoy has invested him with his own

ideas. This is a defect of several of the most
notable types in *War and Peace* and in *Anna
Karenin ;* for example, Prince Andrei, Pierre
Besoukhov, Levine, and others. The fault was less
grave, however, in these earlier books ; for the
characters, by force of their circumstances and their
age, were nearer to the author's actual state of mind.
But in *Resurrection* the author places in the body of
an epicurean of thirty-five the disembodied soul of
an old man of seventy. I will not say that the
moral crisis through which Nekhludov is supposed
to pass is absolutely untrue and impossible ; nor
even that it could not be brought about so
suddenly.[1] But there is nothing in the temperament, the character, the previous life of the man
as Tolstoy depicts him, to announce or explain
this crisis ; and once it has commenced nothing
interrupts it. Tolstoy has, it is true, with profound
observation, represented the impure alloy which at
the outset is mingled with the thoughts of sacrifice ;
the tears of self-pity and admiration ; and, later, the
horror and repugnance which seize upon Nekhludov
when he is brought face to face with reality. But
his resolution never flinches. This crisis has
nothing in common with his previous crises, violent

[1] " Men carry in them the germ of all the human qualities,
and they manifest now one, now another, so that they often
appear to be not themselves ; that is, themselves as they
habitually appear. Among some these changes are more
rare ; among others more rapid. To the second class of men
belongs Nekhludov. Under the influence of various physical
or moral causes sudden and complete changes are incessantly
being produced within him." (*Resurrection.*)

but only momentary.[1] Henceforth nothing can arrest this weak and undecided character. A wealthy prince, much respected, greatly enjoying the good things of the world, on the point of marrying a charming girl who loves him and is not distasteful to him, he suddenly decides to abandon everything—wealth, the world, and social position—and to marry a prostitute in order to atone for a remote offence ; and his exaltation survives, without flinching, for months ; it holds out against every trial, even the news that the woman he wishes to make his wife is continuing her life of debauchery.[2] Here we have a saintliness of which the psychology of a Dostoyevsky would have shown us the source, in the obscure depths of the conscience or even in the organism of his hero. Nekhludov, however, is by no means one of Dostoyevsky's heroes. He is the type of the average man, commonplace, sane, who is Tolstoy's usual hero. To be exact, we are conscious of the

---

[1] " Many times in his life he had proceeded to *clean up his conscience.* This was the term he used to denote those moral crises in which he decided to sweep out the moral refuse which littered his soul. At the conclusion of these crises he never failed to set himself certain rules, which he swore always to keep. He kept a diary ; he began a new life. But each time it was not long before he fell once more to the same level, or lower still, than before the crisis." (*Resurrection.*)

[2] Upon learning that Maslova is engaged in an intrigue with a hospital attendant, Nekhludov is more than ever decided to " sacrifice his liberty in order to redeem the sin of this woman."

juxtaposition of a very materialistic [1] character and a moral crisis which belongs to another man, and that man the aged Tolstoy.

The same impression—one of elemental duality—is again produced at the end of the book, where a third part, full of strictly realistic observation, is set beside an evangelical conclusion which is not in any way essential; it is an act of personal faith,[2] which does not logically issue from the life under observation. This is not the first time that Tolstoy's religion has become involved with his realism; but in previous works the two elements have been better mingled. Here they are not amalgamated; they simply coexist; and the contrast is the more striking in that Tolstoy's faith is always becoming less and less indifferent to proof, while his realism is daily becoming more finely whetted, more free from convention. Here is a sign, not of fatigue, but of age; a certain stiffness, so to speak, in the joints. The religious conclusion is not the organic development of the work. It is a *Deus ex machinâ*. I personally am convinced that right in the depth of

[1] Tolstoy has never drawn a character with so sure, so broad a touch as in the beginning of *Resurrection*. Witness the admirable description of Nekhludov's toilet and his actions of the morning before the first session in the Palace of Justice.

[2] The word "act" to be found here and there in the text in such phrases as "act of faith," "act of will," is used in a sense peculiar to Catholic and Orthodox Christians. A penitent is told to perform an "act of faith" as penance; which is usually the repetition of certain prayers of the nature of a creed. The "act," in short, is a repetition, a declamation, a meditation: anything but an action.—[TRANS.]

Tolstoy's being—in spite of all his affirmations—the fusion between his two diverse natures was by no means complete : between the truth of the artist and the truth of the believer.

Although *Resurrection* has not the harmonious fullness of the work of his youth, and although I, for my part, prefer *War and Peace,* it is none the less one of the most beautiful poems of human compassion ; perhaps the most truthful ever written. More than in any other book I see through the pages of this those bright eyes of Tolstoy's, the pale-grey, piercing eyes, " the look that goes straight to the heart," [1] and in each heart sees its God.

[1] Letter of Countess Tolstoy's, 1884.

XVI

RELIGION
AND
POLITICS

CHAPTER XVI

RELIGION AND POLITICS

TOLSTOY never renounced his art. A great artist
cannot, even if he would, abandon the reason of his
existence. He can, for religious reasons, cease to
publish, but he cannot cease to write. Tolstoy
never interrupted his work of artistic creation.
M. Paul Boyer, who saw him, during the last few
years, at Yasnaya Polyana, says that he would now
give prominence to his evangelistic works, now to
his works of imagination ; he would work at the
one as a relaxation from the other. When he had
finished some social pamphlet, some *Appeal to the
Rulers* or *to the Ruled,* he would allow himself to
resume one of the charming tales which he was, so
to speak, in process of recounting to himself; such
as his *Hadji-Mourad,* a military epic, which celebrated an episode of the wars of the Caucasus and
the resistance of the mountaineers under Schamyl.[1]
Art was still his relaxation, his pleasure ; but he
would have thought it a piece of vanity to make a
parade of it. With the exception of his *Cycle of*

[1] *Le Temps,* November 2, 1902.

Readings for Every Day of the Year (1904–5),[1] in which he collected the thoughts of various writers upon *Life and the Truth*—a true anthology of the poetical wisdom of the world, from the Holy Books of the East to the works of contemporary writers —nearly all his literary works of art, properly so called, which have been written later than 1900 have remained in manuscript.[2]

On the other hand he was boldly and ardently casting his mystical and polemical writings upon the social battlefield. From 1900 to 1910 such

---

[1] Tolstoy regarded this as one of his most important works. " One of my books—*For Every Day*—to which I have the conceit to attach a great importance . . . ." (Letter to Jan Styka, July 27–August 9, 1909).

[2] These works should shortly appear, under the supervision of Countess Alexandra, Tolstoy's daughter. The list of them has been published in various iournals. We may mention *Hadji-Mourad, Father Sergius,* the psychology of a monk ; *She Had Every Virtue,* the study of a woman ; the *Diary of a Madman,* the *Diary of a Mother,* the *Story of a Doukhobor,* the *Story of a Hive,* the *Posthumous Journal of Theodore Kouzmitch, Aliocha Govchkoff, Tikhon and Melanie, After the Ball, The Moon shines in the Dark, A Young Tsar, What I saw in a Dream, Who is the Murderer ?* (containing social ideas), *Modern Socialism,* a comedy ; *The Learned Woman, Childish Wisdom,* sketches of children who converse upon moral subjects ; *The Living Corpse,* a drama in seventeen tableaux ; *It is all her Fault,* a peasant comedy in two acts, directed against alcohol (apparently Tolstoy's last literary work, as he wrote it in May–June, 1910), and a number of social studies. It is announced that they will form two octavo volumes of six hundred pages each.

But the essential work as yet unpublished is Tolstoy's *Journal,* which covers forty years of his life, and will fill, so it is said, no less than thirty volumes.

work absorbed the greater part of his time and
energy. Russia was passing through an alarming
crisis; for a moment the empire of the Tsars seemed
to totter on its foundations and about to fall in ruin.
The Russo-Japanese war, the disasters which followed it, the revolutionary troubles, the mutinies in
the army and the fleet, the massacres, the agrarian
disorders, seemed to mark " the end of a world," to
quote the title of one of Tolstoy's writings. The
height of the crisis was reached in 1904 and 1905.
During these years Tolstoy published a remarkable series of works : *War and Revolution, The
Great Crime, The End of a World.* During
the last ten years of his life he occupied a
situation unique not only in Russia but in the
world. He was alone, a stranger to all the parties,
to all countries, and rejected by his Church, which
had excommunicated him.[1] The logic of his reason
and the revolutionary character of his faith had " led
him to this dilemma ; to live a stranger to other
men, or a stranger to the truth." He recalls the
Russian proverb : " An old man who lies is a rich
man who steals," and he severs himself from mankind
in order to speak the truth. He tells the whole
truth, and to all. The old hunter of lies continues,
unweariedly, to mark down all superstitions, religious or social, and all fetishes. The only exceptions
are the old maleficent powers—the persecutrix, the

---

[1] The excommunication of Tolstoy by the Holy Synod was
declared on February 22, 1901. The excuse was a chapter of
Resurrection relating to Mass and the Eucharist. This chapter
has unhappily been suppressed in the French edition.

Church, and the imperial autocracy. Perhaps his
enmity towards them was in some degree appeased
now that all were casting stones at them. They
were familiar ; therefore they were already not so
formidable ! After all, too, the Church and the
Tsar were carrying on their peculiar trades ; they
were at least not deceptive. Tolstoy, in his letter to
the Tsar Nikolas II.,[1] although he speaks the truth in
a manner entirely unaccommodating to the man as
sovereign, is full of gentleness for the sovereign as
man ; addressing him as " dear brother," praying him
to " pardon him if he has hurt him unintentionally,"
and signing himself, " Your brother who wishes
you true happiness."

What Tolstoy can least find it in him to pardon—
what he denounces with the utmost hatred—are the
new lies ; not the old ones, which are no longer
able to deceive ; not despotism, but the illusion of
liberty. It is difficult to say which he hates the
more among the followers of the newer idols :
whether the Socialists or the " Liberals."

He had a long-standing antipathy for the Liberals. It had seized upon him suddenly when, as
an officer fresh from Sebastopol, he found himself
in the society of the literary men of St. Petersburg.
It had been one of the causes of his misunderstanding with Tourgenev. The arrogant noble, the man
of ancient race, could not support these " intellectuals," with their profession of making the nation
happy, whether by its will or against it, by forcing
their Utopian schemes upon it. Very much a

[1] On the nationalisation of the soil. (*The Great Crime*, 1905.)

Russian, and of the old stamp,[1] he instinctively
distrusted all liberal innovations, and the constitutional ideas which came from the West ; and his
two journeys abroad only intensified his prejudices.
On his return from his first journey he wrote :

" To avoid the ambition of Liberalism."

On his return from the second :

" A privileged society has no right whatsoever to
educate in its own way the masses of which it
knows nothing."

In *Anna Karenin* he freely expresses his contempt
for Liberals in general. Levine refuses to associate
himself with the work of the provincial institutions
for educating the people, and the innovations which
are the order of the day. The picture of the elections to the provincial assembly exposes the fool's
bargain by which the country changes its ancient
Conservative administration for a Liberal *régime*—
nothing is really altered, except that there is one lie
the more, while the masters are of inferior blood.

" We are not worth very much perhaps," says the
representative of the aristocracy, " but none the less
we have lasted a thousand years."

Tolstoy fulminates against the manner in which
the Liberals abuse the words, " The People : The
Will of the People." What do they know of the
people ? Who are the People ?

But it is more especially when the Liberal movement seemed on the point of succeeding and
achieving the convocation of the first Duma that

[1] " A ' Great-Russian,' touched with Finnish blood." (M.
Leroy-Beaulieu.)

Tolstoy expressed most violently his disapprobation of its constitutional ideas.

" During the last few years the deformation of Christianity has given rise to a new species of fraud, which has rooted our peoples yet more firmly in their servility. With the help of a complicated system of parliamentary elections it was suggested to them that by electing their representatives directly they were participating in the government, and that in obeying them they were obeying their own will : in short, that they were free. This is a piece of imposture. The people cannot express its will, even with the aid of universal suffrage—1, because no such collective will of a nation of many millions of inhabitants could exist ; 2, because even if it existed the majority of voices would not be its expression. Without insisting on the fact that those elected would legislate and administrate not for the general good but in order to maintain themselves in power —without counting on the fact of the popular corruption due to pressure and electoral corruption— this fraud is particularly harmful because of the presumptuous slavery into which all those who submit to it fall. . . . These free men recall the prisoners who imagine that they are enjoying freedom when they have the right to elect those of their gaolers who are entrusted with the interior policing of the prison. . . . A member of a despotic State may be entirely free, even in the midst of the most brutal violence. But a member of a constitutional State is always a slave, for he recognises the legality of the violence done him. . . . And now men wish

to lead the Russian people into the same state of
constitutional slavery in which the other European
peoples dwell ! " [1]

In his hostility towards Liberalism contempt was
his dominant feeling. In respect of Socialism his

[1] *The End of a World* (1905-6). See the telegram addressed
by Tolstoy to an American journal : " The agitation in the
Zemstvos has as its object the limitation of despotic power
and the establishment of a representative government.
Whether or no they succeed the result will be a postpone-
ment of any true social improvement. Political agitation,
while producing the unfortunate illusion of such improvement
by external means, arrests true progress, as may be proved by
the example of all the constitutional States—France, England,
America, &c." (Preface to the French translation of *The Great
Crime*, 1905.)
In a long and interesting letter to a lady who asked him
to join a *Committee for the Propagation of Reading and
Writing among the People,* Tolstoy expressed yet other
objections to the Liberals : they have always played the
part of dupes ; they act as the accomplices of the autocracy
through fear ; their participation in the government gives the
latter a moral prestige, and accustoms them to compromises,
which quickly make them the instruments of power.
Alexander II. used to say that all the Liberals were ready to
sell themselves for honours if not for money ; Alexander III.
was able, without danger, to eradicate the liberal work of his
father. " The Liberals whispered among themselves that this
did not please them ; but they continued to attend the
tribunals, to serve the State and the press ; in the press they
alluded to those things to which allusion was allowed, and
were silent upon matters to which allusion was prohibited."
They did the same under Nikolas II. " When this young
man, who knows nothing and understands nothing, replies
tactlessly and with effrontery to the representatives of the
people, do the Liberals protest ? By no means . . . From
every side they send the young Tsar their cowardly and
flattering congratulations." (*Further Letters.*)

dominant feeling was—or rather would have been—
hatred, if Tolstoy had not forbidden himself to hate
anything whatever. He detested it doubly, because
Socialism was the amalgamation of two lies : the lie
of liberty and the lie of science. Does it not profess
to be founded upon some sort of economic science,
whose laws absolutely rule the progress of the world ?

Tolstoy is very hard upon science. He has
pages full of terrible irony concerning this modern
superstition and "these futile problems : the origin
of species, spectrum analysis, the nature of radium,
the theory of numbers, animal fossils and other
nonsense, to which people attach as much importance to-day as they attributed in the Middle Ages
to the Immaculate Conception or the Duality of
Substance." He derides these "servants of science,
who, just as the servants of the Church, per-
suade themselves and others that they are saving
humanity ; who, like the Church, believe in their
own infallibility, never agree among themselves,
divide themselves into sects, and, like the Church,
are the chief cause of unmannerliness, moral
ignorance, and the long delay of humanity in
freeing itself from the evils under which it suffers ;
for they have rejected the only thing that could
unite humanity : the religious conscience." [1]

[1] *War and Revolution.*

In *Resurrection*, at the hearing of Maslova's appeal, in the
Senate, it is a materialistic Darwinist who is most strongly
opposed to the revision, because he is secretly shocked that
Nekhludov should wish, as a matter of duty, to marry a prostitute ; any manifestation of duty, and still more, of religious
feeling, having the effect upon him of a personal insult.

But his anxiety redoubles, and his indignation bursts its bounds, when he sees the dangerous weapon of the new fanaticism in the hands of those who profess to be regenerating humanity. Every revolutionist saddens him when he resorts to violence. But the intellectual and theoretical revolutionary inspires him with horror : he is a pedantic murderer, an arrogant, sterile intelligence, who loves not men but ideas.[1]

Moreover, these ideas are of a low order.

" The object of Socialism is the satisfaction of the lowest needs of man : his material well-being. And it cannot attain even this end by the means it recommends." [2]

At heart, he is without love. He feels only hatred for the oppressors and "a black envy for the assured and easy life of the rich : a greed like that of the flies that gather about ordure." [3]   When

[1] As a type, take Novodvorov, the revolutionary leader in *Resurrection*, whose excessive vanity and egoism have sterilised a fine intelligence. No imagination ; "a total absence of the moral and æsthetic qualities which produce doubt."

Following his footsteps like a shadow is Markel, the artisan who has become a revolutionist through humiliation and the desire for revenge ; a passionate worshipper of science, which he cannot comprehend ; a fanatical anti-clerical and an ascetic.

In *Three More Dead* or *The Divine and the Human* we shall find a few specimens of the new generation of revolutionaries : Romane and his friends, who despise the old Terrorists, and profess to attain their ends scientifically, by transforming an agricultural into an industrial people.

[2] Letters to the Japanese Izo-Abe, 1904.   (*Further Letters.*)

[3] Conversations, reported by Teneromo (published in *Revolutionaries*, 1906).

Socialism is victorious the aspect of the world will be terrible. The European horde will rush upon the weak and barbarous peoples with redoubled force, and will enslave them, in order that the ancient proletariats of Europe may debauch themselves at their leisure by idle luxury, as did the people of Rome.[1]

Happily the principal energies of Socialism spend themselves in smoke—in speeches, like those of M. Jaurès.

"What an admirable orator ! There is something of everything in his speeches—and there is nothing. . . . Socialism is a little like our Russian orthodoxy : you press it, you push it into its last trenches, you think you have got it fast, and suddenly it turns round and tells you : ' No, I'm not the one you think, I'm somebody else.' And it slips out of your hands. . . . Patience ! Let time do its work. There will be socialistic theories, as there are women's fashions, which soon pass from the drawing-room to the servants' hall."[2]

Although Tolstoy waged war in this manner upon the Liberals and Socialists, it was not—far from it—to leave the field free for autocracy ; on the contrary, it was that the battle might be fought in all its fierceness between the old world and the new, after the army of disorderly and dangerous elements had been eliminated. For Tolstoy too was a believer in the Revolution. But his Revolu-

[1] Conversations, reported by Teneromo (published in *Revolutionaries*, 1906).

[2] Conversation with M. Paul Boyer. (*Le Temps*, November 4, 1902.)

tion was of a very different colour to that of the
revolutionaries ; it was rather that of a believer of the
Middle Ages, who looked on the morrow, perhaps
that very day, for the reign of the Holy Spirit.

" I believe that at this very hour the great
revolution is beginning which has been preparing
for two thousand years in the Christian world—
the revolution which will substitute for corrupted
Christianity and the system of domination which
proceeds therefrom the true Christianity, the basis
of equality between men and of the true liberty
to which all beings endowed with reason aspire." [1]

What time does he choose, this seer and prophet,
for his announcement of the new era of love and
happiness ?   The darkest hour of Russian history ;
the hour of disaster and of shame !   Superb power
of creative faith !   All around it is light—even in
darkness.   Tolstoy saw in death the signs of re-
newal ; in the calamities of the war in Manchuria, in
the downfall of the Russian armies, in the frightful
anarchy and the bloody struggle of the classes.   His
logic—the logic of a dream !—drew from the victory
of Japan the astonishing conclusion that Russia
should withdraw from all warfare, because the non-
Christian peoples will always have the advantage
in warfare over the Christian peoples " who have
passed through the phase of servile submission."
Does this mean the abdication of the Russian
people ?   No ; this is pride at its supremest.
Russia should withdraw from all warfare because
she must accomplish "the great revolution."

[1] *The End of a World.*

"The Revolution of 1905, which will set men free from brutal oppression, must commence in Russia. It is beginning."

Why must Russia play the part of the chosen people ? Because the new Revolution must before all repair the "Great Crime," the great monopolisation of the soil for the profit of a few thousands of wealthy men and the slavery of millions of men— the cruellest of enslavements ; [1] and because no people was so conscious of this iniquity as the Russian people.[2]

---

[1] "The cruellest enslavement is to be deprived of the earth, for the slave of a master is the slave of only one ; but the man deprived of the land is the slave of all the world." (*The Great Crime.*)

[2] Russia was actually in a somewhat special situation ; and although Tolstoy may have been wrong to found his generalisations concerning other European States upon the condition of Russia, we cannot be surprised that he was most sensible to the sufferings which touched him most nearly. See, in *The Great Crime*, his conversations on the road to Toula with the peasants, who were all in want of bread because they lacked land, and who were all secretly waiting for the land to be restored to them. The agricultural population of Russia forms 80 per cent. of the nation. A hundred million of men, says Tolstoy, are dying of hunger because of the seizure of the soil by the landed proprietors. When people speak to them of remedying their evils through the agency of the Press, or by the separation of Church and State, or by nationalist representation, or even by the eight-hours day, they impudently mock at them :

"Those who are apparently looking everywhere for the means of bettering the condition of the masses of the people remind one of what one sees in the theatre, when all the spectators have an excellent view of an actor who is supposed to be concealed, while his fellow-players, who also have a full

Again, and more especially, because the Russian
people is of all peoples most thoroughly steeped in
the true Christianity, so that the coming revolution
should realise, in the name of Christ, the law of
union and of love. Now this law of love cannot
be fulfilled unless it is based upon the law of
non-resistance to evil.[1] This non-resistance (let
us mark this well, we who have the misfortune
to see in it simply an Utopian fad peculiar to
Tolstoy and to a few dreamers) has always been
an essential trait of the Russian people.

"The Russian people has always assumed, with
regard to power, an attitude entirely strange to the
other peoples of Europe. It has never entered
upon a conflict with power ; it has never partici-
pated in it, and consequently has never been
depraved by it. It has regarded power as an evil
which must be avoided. An ancient legend represents the Russians as appealing to the Varingians
to come and govern them. The majority of the

view of him, pretend not to see him, and endeavour to distract
one another's attention from him."

There is no remedy but that of returning the soil to the
labouring people. As a solution of the property question,
Tolstoy recommends the doctrine of Henry George and his
suggested single tax upon the value of the soil. This is his
economic gospel ; he returns to it unwearied, and has
assimilated it so thoroughly that in his writings he often
uses entire phrases of George's.

[1] "The law of non-resistance to evil is the keystone of the
whole building. To admit the law of mutual help while
misunderstanding the precept of non-resistance is to build
the vault without sealing the central portion." (*The End of
a World.*)

Russians have always preferred to submit to acts of violence rather than respond with violence or participate therein. They have therefore always submitted.

"A voluntary submission, having nothing in common with servile obedience.[1]

"The true Christian may submit, indeed it is impossible for him not to submit without a struggle to no matter what violence; but he could not obey it—that is, he could not recognise it as legitimate." [2]

At the time of writing these lines Tolstoy was still subject to the emotion caused by one of the most tragical examples of this heroic non-resistance of a people—the bloody manifestation of January 22nd in St. Petersburg, when an unarmed crowd, led by Father Gapon, allowed itself to be shot down without a cry of hatred or a gesture of self-defence.

For a long time the Old Believers, known in Russia as the *Sectators*, had been obstinately practising, in spite of persecution, non-obedience to the State, and had refused to recognise the legitimacy of its power.[3] The absurdity of the Russo-Japanese

[1] In a letter written in 1900 to a friend (*Further Letters*) Tolstoy complains of the false interpretation given to his doctrine of non-resistance. People, he says, confound *Do not oppose evil by evil* with *Do not oppose evil* : that is to say, *Be indifferent to evil. . . ."* "Whereas the conflict with evil is the sole object of Christianity, and the commandment of non-resistance to evil is given as the most effectual means of conflict."

[2] *The End of a World.*

[3] Tolstoy has drawn two types of these "Sectators," one in *Resurrection* (towards the end) and one in *Three More Dead.*

war enabled this state of mind to spread without difficulty through the rural districts. Refusals of military service became more and more general; and the more brutally they were punished the more stubborn the revolt grew in secret. In the provinces, moreover, whole races who knew nothing of Tolstoy had given the example of an absolute and passive refusal to obey the State—the Doukhobors of the Caucasus as early as 1898 and the Georgians of the Gouri towards 1905. Tolstoy influenced these movements far less than they influenced him; and the interest of his writings lies in the fact that in spite of the criticisms of those writers who were of the party of revolution, as was Gorky,[1] he was the mouthpiece of the Old Russian people.

The attitude which he preserved, in respect of men who at the peril of their lives were putting into practice the principles which he professed,[2] was one of extreme modesty and dignity. Neither to the

---

[1] After Tolstoy's condemnation of the upheaval in the Zemstvos, Gorky, making himself the interpreter of the displeasure of his friends, wrote as follows : " This man has become the slave of his theory. For a long time he has isolated himself from the life of Russia, and he no longer listens to the voice of the people. He hovers over Russia at too great a height."

[2] It was a bitter trial to him that he could not contrive to be persecuted. He had a thirst for martyrdom ; but the Government very wisely took good care not to satisfy him.

" They are persecuting my friends all around me, and leaving me in peace, although if any one is dangerous it is I. Evidently I am not worth persecution, and I am ashamed of the fact." (Letter to Teneromo, 1892, *Further Letters*.)

" Evidently I am not worthy of persecution, and I shall have

Doukhobors and the Gourians nor to the refractory soldiers did he assume the pose of a master or teacher.

" He who suffers no trials can teach nothing to him who does so suffer."

He implores "the forgiveness of all those whom his words and his writings may have caused to suffer."[1]

He never urges any one to refuse military service. It is a matter for every man to decide for himself. If he discusses the matter with any one who is hesitating, " he always advises him not to refuse obedience so long as it would not be morally impossible." For if a man hesitates it is because he is not ripe ; and " it is better to have one soldier the more than a regenade or hypocrite, which is what becomes of those who undertake a task beyond their

to die like this, without having ever been able to testify to the truth by physical suffering." (To Teneromo, May 16, 1892, *ibid.*)

"It hurts me to be at liberty." (To Teneromo, June 1, 1894, *ibid.*)

That he was at liberty was, Heaven knows, no fault of his ! He insults the Tsars, he attacks the fatherland, "that ghastly fetish to which men sacrifice their life and liberty and reason." (*The End of a World.*) Then see, in *War and Revolution*, the summary of Russian history. It is a gallery of monsters : "The maniac Ivan the Terrible, the drunkard Peter I., the ignorant cook, Catherine I., the sensual and profligate Elizabeth, the degenerate Paul, the parricide Alexander I. [the only one of them for whom Tolstoy felt a secret liking], the cruel and ignorant Nikolas I. ; Alexander II., unintelligent and evil rather than good ; Alexander III., an undeniable sot, brutal and ignorant; Nikolas II., an innocent young officer of hussars, with an *entourage* of coxcombs, a young man who knows nothing and understands nothing."

[1] Letter to Gontcharenko, a "refractory," January 17, 1903. (*Further Letters.*)

strength." [1]   He distrusts the resolution of the
refractory Gontcharenko. He fears "that this young
man may have been carried away by vanity and
vainglory, not by the love of God." [2]   To the Doukhobors he writes that they should not persist in
their refusal of obedience out of pride, but "if they
are capable of so doing, they should save their weaker
women and their children. No one will blame them
for that." They must persist "only if the spirit of
Christ is indeed within them, because then they will
be happy to suffer." [3] In any case he prays those
who are persecuted "at any cost not to break their
affectionate relations with those who persecute
them." [4]   One must love even Herod, as he says in
a letter to a friend : "You say, 'One cannot love
Herod.'—I do not know, but I feel, and you also, that
one must love him. I know, and you also, that if I
do not love him I suffer, that there is no life in me." [5]

The Divine purity, the unvarying ardour of this
love, which in the end can no longer be contented
even by the words of the Gospel : " Love thy neighbour as thyself," because he finds in them a taint of
egoism ! [6]

---

[1] Letter to a friend, 1900. (*Correspondence.*)

[2] To Gontcharenko, February 2, 1903 (*ibid.*).

[3] To the Doukhobors of the Caucasus, 1898 (*ibid.*).

[4] To Gontcharenko, January 17, 1903 (*ibid.*).

[5] To a friend, November, 1901. (*Correspondence.*)

[6] " It is like a crack in a pneumatic machine ; all the vapour
of egoism that we wish to drain from the human soul re-enters
by it." He ingeniously strives to prove that the original text
has been wrongly read ; that the exact wording of the Second
Commandment was in fact " Love thy neighbour as *Himself*
(as God)." (*Conversations with Teneromo.*)

Too vast a love in the opinion of some ; and so free from human egoism that it wastes itself in the void. Yet who more than Tolstoy distrusts "abstract love" ?

"The greatest modern sin : the abstract love of humanity, impersonal love for those who are— somewhere, out of sight. . . . To love those we do not know, those whom we shall never meet, is so easy a thing ! There is no need to sacrifice any- thing ; and at the same time we are so pleased with ourselves ! The conscience is fooled.—No. We must love our neighbours—those we live with, and who are in our way and embarrass us." [1]

I have read in most of the studies of Tolstoy's work that his faith and philosophy are not original. It is true ; the beauty of these ideas is eternal and can never appear a momentary fashion. Others complain of their Utopian character. This also is true ; they are Utopian, the New Testament is Utopian. A prophet is a Utopian ; he treads the earth but sees the life of eternity ; and that this apparition should have been granted to us, that we should have seen among us the last of the prophets, that the greatest of our artists should wear this aureole on his brow—there, it seems to me, is a fact more novel and of far greater importance to the world than one religion the more, or a new philosophy. Those are blind who do not perceive the miracle of this great mind, the incarnation of fraternal love in the midst of a people and a century stained with the blood of hatred !

[1] *Conversations with Teneromo.*

XVII

OLD AGE

CHAPTER XVII

OLD AGE

His face had taken on definite lines; had become as it will remain in the memory of men: the large countenance, crossed by the arch of a double furrow; the white, bristling eyebrows; the patri-archal beard, recalling that of the Moses of Dijon. The aged face was gentler and softer; it bore the traces of illness, of sorrow, of disappointment, and of affectionate kindness. What a change from the almost animal brutality of the same face at twenty, and the heavy rigidity of the soldier of Sebastopol! But the eyes have always the same profound fixity, the same look of loyalty, which hides nothing and from which nothing is hidden.

Nine years before his death, in his reply to the Holy Synod (April 17, 1901) Tolstoy had said:

"I owe it to my faith to live in peace and gladness, and to be able also, in peace and gladness, to travel on towards death."

Reading this I am reminded of the ancient saying: "that we should call no man happy until he is dead."

Were they lasting, this peace and joy that he then boasted of possessing ?

The hopes of the " great Revolution" of 1905 had vanished. The shadows had gathered more thickly ; the expected light had never risen. To the upheavals of the revolutionaries exhaustion had succeeded. Nothing of the old injustice was altered, except that poverty had increased. Even in 1906 Tolstoy had lost a little of his confidence in the historic vocation of the Russian Slavs, and his obstinate faith sought abroad for other peoples whom he might invest with this mission. He thought of the "great and wise Chinese nation." He believed "that the peoples of the Orient were called to recover that liberty which the peoples of the Occident had lost almost without chance of recovery"; and that China, at the head of the Asiatic peoples, would accomplish the transformation of humanity in the way of Tao, the eternal Law.[1]

A hope quickly destroyed : the China of Lao-Tse and Confucius was decrying its bygone wisdom, as Japan had already done in order to imitate Europe.[2] The persecuted Doukhobors had migrated to Canada, and there, to the scandal of Tolstoy, they immediately reverted to the property system.[3]   The

[1] Letter to the Chinese, October, 1906. (*Further Letters.*)

[2] Tolstoy expressed a fear that this might happen in the above letter.

[3] " It was hardly worth while to refuse military and police service only to revert to property, which is maintained only by those two services. Those who enter the service and profit by property act better than those who refuse all service and enjoy property." (Letter to the Doukhobors of Canada, 1899. *Further Letters.*)

Gourians were scarcely delivered from the yoke of
the State when they began to destroy those who did
not think as they did ; and the Russian troops were
called out to put matters in order. The very Jews,
"whose native country had hitherto been the fairest
a man could desire—the Book,"[1] were attacked by
the malady of Zionism, that movement of false
nationalism, "which is flesh of the flesh of contemporary Europeanism, or rather its rickety child."[2]

Tolstoy was saddened, but not discouraged. He
had faith in God and in the future.

"All would be perfect if one could grow a forest
in the wink of an eye. Unhappily, this is impossible ; we must wait until the seed germinates,
until the shoots push up, the leaves come, and then
the stem which finally becomes a tree."[3]

But many trees are needed to make a forest ; and
Tolstoy was alone ; glorious, but alone. Men wrote
to him from all parts of the world ; from Mohame-
dan countries, from China and Japan, where *Resurrection* was translated, and where his ideas upon
"the restitution of the land to the people" were
being propagated.[4] The American papers inter-

[1] In the *Conversations with Teneromo* there is a fine page
dealing with "the wise Jew, who, immersed in this Book, has
not seen the centuries crumble above his head, nor the peoples
that appear and disappear from the face of the earth."

[2] To see the progress of Europe in the horrors of the
modern State, the bloodstained State, and to wish to create a
new *Judenstaat* is an abominable sin." (*Ibid.*)

[3] *Appeal to Political Men*, 1905.

[4] In the appendix to *The Great Crime* and in the French
translation of *Advice to the Ruled* is the appeal of a Japanese
society for the *Re-establishment of the Liberty of the Earth*.

viewed him; the French consulted him on matters of art, or the separation of Church and State.[1]

But he had not three hundred disciples, and he knew it. Moreover, he did not take pains to make them. He repulsed the attempts of his friends to form groups of Tolstoyans.

"We must not go in search of one another, but we must all seek God. . . . You say: 'Together it is easier.'—What? To labour, to reap, yes. But to draw near to God—one can only do so in isolation. . . . I see the world as an enormous temple in which the light falls from on high and precisely in the middle. To become united we must all go towards the light. Then all of us, come together from all directions, will find ourselves in the company of men we did not look for; in that is the joy."[2]

How many have found themselves together under the ray which falls from the dome? What matter! It is enough to be one and alone if one is with God.

"As only a burning object can communicate fire to other objects, so only the true faith and life of a man can communicate themselves to other men and to spread the truth."[3]

Perhaps; but to what point was this isolated faith able to assure Tolstoy of happiness? How far he

[1] Letter to Paul Sabatier, November 7, 1906. (*Further Letters.*)

[2] Letters to Teneromo, June, 1882, and to a friend, November, 1901. (*Further Letters.*)

[3] *War and Revolution.*

was, in his latter days, from the voluntary calm of a Goethe! One would almost say that he avoided it, fled from it, hated it.

"One must thank God for being discontented with oneself. If one could always be so! The discord of life with what ought to be is precisely the sign of life itself, the movement upwards from the lesser to the greater, from worse to better. And this discord is the condition of good. It is an evil when a man is calm and satisfied with himself."[1]

He imagines the following subject for a novel— showing that the persistent discontent of a Levine or a Besoukhov was not yet extinct in him:

"I often picture to myself a man brought up in revolutionary circles, and at first a revolutionist, then a populist, then a socialist, then orthodox, then a monk at Afone, then an atheist, a good paterfamilias, and finally a Doukhobor. He takes up everything and is always forsaking everything; men deride him, for he has performed nothing, and dies, forgotten, in a hospital. Dying, he thinks he has wasted his life. And yet he is a saint."[2]

Had he still doubts—he, so full of faith? Who knows? In a man who has remained robust in body and mind even into old age life cannot come to a halt at a definite stage of thought. Life goes onwards.

"Movement is life."[3]

[1] *War and Revolution.*

[2] Perhaps this refers to the History of a Doukhobor, the title of which figures in the list of Tolstoy's unpublished works.

[3] "Suppose that all the men who had the truth were to be installed all together on an island. Would that be life?" (To a friend, March, 1901. *Further Letters.*)

Many things must have changed within him
during the last few years. Did he not modify his
opinion of revolutionaries ? Who can even say
that his faith in non-resistance to evil was not
at length a little shaken ? Even in *Resurrection*
the relations of Nekhludov with the condemned
"politicals" completely change his ideas as to the
Russian revolutionary party.

"Up till that time he had felt an aversion for
their cruelty, their criminal dissimulation, their
attempts upon life, their sufficiency, their self-
contentment, their insupportable vanity. But when
he saw them more closely, when he saw how they
were treated by the authorities, he understood that
they could not be otherwise."

And he admires their high ideal of duty, which
implies total self-sacrifice.

Since 1900, however, the revolutionary tide had
risen ; starting from the "intellectuals," it had
gained the people, and was obscurely moving
amidst the thousands of the poor. The advance-
guard of their threatening army defiled below
Tolstoy's window at Yasnaya Polyana. Three tales,
published by the *Mercure de France*,[1] which were
among the last pages written by Tolstoy, give us a
glimpse of the sorrow and the perplexity which
this spectacle caused him. The years were indeed
remote when the pilgrims wandered through the
countryside of Toula, pious and simple of heart.
Now he saw the invasion of starving wanderers.
They came to him every day. Tolstoy, who chatted

[1] December 1, 1910.

with them, was struck by the hatred that animated
them ; they no longer, as before, saw the rich as
"people who save their souls by distributing alms,
but as bandits, brigands, who drink the blood of
the labouring people." Many were educated men,
ruined, on the brink of that despair which makes a
man capable of anything.

"It is not in the deserts and the forests, but in
slums of cities and on the great highways that the
barbarians are reared who will do to modern
civilisation what the Huns and Vandals did to the
ancient civilisation."

So said Henry George. And Tolstoy adds :

"The Vandals are already here in Russia, and
they will be particularly terrible among our profoundly religious people, because we know nothing
of the curbs, the *convenances* and public opinion,
which are so strongly developed among European
peoples."

Tolstoy often received letters from these rebels,
protesting against his doctrine of non-resistance to
evil, and saying that the evil that the rulers and the
wealthy do to the people can only be replied to
by cries of "Vengeance ! Vengeance ! Vengeance !"
Did Tolstoy still condemn them ? We do not
know. But when, a few days later, he saw in his
own village the villagers weeping while their sheep
and their samovars were seized and taken from
them by callous authorities, he also cried vengeance
in vain against these thieves, " these ministers
and their acolytes, who are engaged in the brandy
traffic, or in teaching men to murder, or condemning

men to deportation, prison, or the gallows—these men, all perfectly convinced that the samovars, sheep, calves, and linen which they took from the miserable peasants would find their highest use in furthering the distillation of brandy which poisons the drinker, in the manufacture of murderous weapons, in the construction of jails and convict prisons, and above all in the distribution of appointments to their assistants and themselves."

It is sad, after a whole life lived in the expectation and the proclamation of the reign of love, to be forced to close ones eye's in the midst of these threatening visions, and to feel one's whole position crumbling. It is still sadder for one with the impeccably truthful conscience of a Tolstoy to be forced to confess to oneself that one's life has not been lived entirely in accordance with one's principles.

Here we touch upon the most pitiful point of these latter years—should we say of the last thirty years ?—and we can only touch upon it with a pious and tentative hand, for this sorrow, of which Tolstoy endeavoured to keep the secret, belongs not only to him who is dead, but to others who are living, whom he loved, and who loved him.

He was never able to communicate his faith to those who were dearest to him—his wife and children. We have seen how the loyal comrade, who had so valiantly shared his artistic life and labour, suffered when he denied his faith in art for a different and a moral faith, which she did not understand. Tolstoy suffered no less at feel-

ing that he was misunderstood by his nearest
friend.

" I feel in all my being," he wrote to Teneromo,
" the truth of these words : that the husband and
the wife are not separate beings, but are as one. . . .
I wish most earnestly that I had the power to
transmit to my wife a portion of that religious
conscience which gives me the possibility of sometimes raising myself above the sorrows of life.
I hope that it will be given her ; very probably not
by me, but by God, although this conscience is
hardly accessible to women." [1]

It seems that this wish was never gratified.
Countess Tolstoy loved and admired the purity of
heart, the candid heroism, and the goodness of the
great man who was " as one " with her ; she saw
that " he marched ahead of the host and showed
men the way they should follow" ; [2] when the
Holy Synod excommunicated him she bravely
undertook his defence and insisted on sharing the
danger which threatened him. But she could not
force herself to believe what she did not believe ;
and Tolstoy was too sincere to urge her to
pretend—he who loathed the petty deceits of faith
and love even more than the negation of faith and
love.[3] How then could he constrain her, not

---

[1] May 16, 1892. Tolstoy's wife was then mourning the
loss of a little boy, and he could do nothing to console her.

[2] Letter of January, 1883.

[3] " I should never reproach any one for having no religion.
The shocking thing is when men lie and pretend to religion."
And further : " May God preserve us from pretending to love ;
it is worse than hatred."

believing, to modify her life, to sacrifice her fortune and that of her children ?

With his children the rift was wider still. M. Leroy-Beaulieu, who saw Tolstoy with his family at Yasnaya Polyana, says that " at table, when the father was speaking, the sons barely concealed their weariness and unbelief." [1] His faith had only slightly affected two or three of his daughters, of whom one, Marie, was dead. He was morally isolated in the heart of his family." " He had scarcely any one but his youngest daughter and his doctor " [2] to understand him.

He suffered from this mental loneliness ; and he suffered from the social relations which were forced upon him ; the reception of fatiguing visitors from every quarter of the globe ; Americans, and the idly curious, who wore him out ; he suffered from the " luxury " in which his family life forced him to live. It was a modest luxury, if we are to believe the accounts of those who saw him in his simple house, with its almost austere appointments ; in his little room, with its iron bed, its cheap chairs, and its naked walls ! But even this poor comfort weighed upon him ; it was a cause of perpetual remorse. In the second of the tales published by the *Mercure de France* he bitterly contrasts the spectacle of the poverty about him with the luxury of his own house.

" My activity," he wrote as early as 1903, " however useful it may appear to certain people, loses

[1] *Revue des Deux Mondes*, December 15, 1910.
[2] *Ibid.*

the greater part of its importance by the fact
that my life is not entirely in agreement with my
professions." [1]

Why did he not realise this agreement ? If he
could not induce his family to cut themselves off
from the world, why did he not leave them, go
out of their life, thus avoiding the sarcasm and
the reproach of hypocrisy expressed by his enemies,
who were only too glad to follow his example and
make it an excuse for denying his doctrines ?

He had thought of so doing. For a long time he
was quite resolved. A remarkable letter [2] of his has
recently been found and published ; it was written
to his wife on the 8th of June, 1897. The greater
part of it is printed below. Nothing could better
express the secret of this loving and unhappy heart :

"For a long time, dear Sophie, I have been
suffering from the discord between my life and my
beliefs. I cannot force you to change your life or
your habits. Neither have I hitherto been able to
leave you, for I felt that by my departure I should
deprive the children, still very young, of the little
influence I might be able to exert over them, and
also that I should cause you all a great deal of pain.
But I cannot continue to live as I have lived during
these last sixteen years,[3] now struggling against you
and irritating you, now succumbing myself to the

---

[1] To a friend, December 10, 1903.

[2] *Figaro*, December 27, 1910. It was found among
Tolstoy's papers after his death.

[3] This state of suffering dates, as we see, from 1881 ; that is,
from the winter passed in Moscow, and Tolstoy's discovery of
social wretchedness.

influences and the seductions to which I am accustomed and which surround me. I have resolved now to do what I have wished to do for a long time : to go away. . . . Just as the Hindoos, when they arrive at their sixtieth year, go away into the forest ; just as every aged and religious man wishes to consecrate the last years of his life to God and not to jesting, punning, family tittle-tattle, and lawn-tennis ; so do I with all my strength desire peace and solitude, and, if not an absolute harmony, at least not this crying discord between my whole life and my conscience. If I had gone away openly there would have been supplications, discussions, arguments ; I should have weakened, and perhaps I should not have carried out my decision, and it ought to be carried out. I beg you therefore to forgive me if my action grieves you. And you in particular, Sophie—let me go, do not try to find me, do not be angry with me, and do not blame me. The fact that I have left you does not prove that I have any grievance against you. . . . I know that you *could not, could not* see and think with me ; this is why you could not change your life, could not sacrifice yourself to something you did not understand. I do not blame you at all ; on the contrary, I remember with love and gratitude the thirty-five long years of our life together, and above all the first half of that period, when, with the courage and devotion of your mother's nature, you valiantly fulfilled what you saw as your mission. You have given to me and the world what you had to give. You have given much maternal love and made great sacrifices.

. . . But in the latter period of our life, in the last fifteen years, our paths have lain apart. I cannot believe that I am the guilty one ; I know that I have changed ; it was not your doing, nor the world's ; it was because I could not do otherwise. I cannot blame you for not having followed me, and I shall always remember with love what you have given me. . . . Goodbye, my dear Sophie. I love you."

"*The fact that I have left you.*" He did not leave her. Poor letter ! It seemed to him that it was enough to write, and his resolution would be fulfilled. . . . Having written, his resolution was already exhausted. "If I had gone away openly there would have been supplications, I should have weakened." . . . There was no need of supplications, of discussion ; it was enough for him to see, a moment later, those whom he wished to leave ; he felt that he *could not, could not* leave them ; and he took the letter in his pocket and buried it among his papers, with this subscription :

"Give this, after my death, to my wife Sophie Andreyevna."

And this was the end of his plan of departure. Was he not strong enough ? Was he not capable of sacrificing his affections to his God ? In the Christian annals there is no lack of saints with tougher hearts, who never hesitated to trample fearlessly underfoot both their own affections and those of others. But how could he ? He was not of their company ; he was weak : he was a man ; and it is for that reason that we love him.

More than fifteen years earlier, on a page full of

heart-breaking wretchedness, he had asked himself :
" Well, Leo Tolstoy, are you living according to
the principles you profess ? "

He replied miserably :

" I am dying of shame ; I am guilty ; I am contemptible. . . . Yet compare my former life with
my life of to-day. You will see that I am trying to
live according to the laws of God. I have not done
the thousandth part of what I ought to do, and I am
confused ; but I have failed to do it not because
I did not wish to do it, but because I could not.
. . . Blame me, but not the path I am taking. If
I know the road to my house, and if I stagger along
it like a drunken man, does that show that the road
is bad ? Show me another, or follow me along the
true path, as I am ready to follow you. But do not
discourage me, do not rejoice in my distress, do not
joyfully cry out : ' Look ! He said he was going to
the house, and he is falling into the ditch ! ' No,
do not be glad, but help me, support me ! . . . Help
me ! My heart is torn with despair lest we should
all be astray ; and when I make every effort to
escape you, at each effort, instead of having compassion, point at me with your finger crying, ' Look,
he is falling into the ditch with us ! ' " [1]

When death was nearer, he wrote once more :

" I am not a saint : I have never professed to be
one. I am a man who allows himself to be carried
away, and who often does not say all that he thinks
and feels ; not because he does not want to, but

[1] Letter to a friend, 1895 (the French version being
published in *Plaisirs cruels*, 1895).

because he cannot, because it often happens that he exaggerates or is mistaken. In my actions it is still worse. I am altogether a weak man with vicious habits, who wishes to serve the God of truth, but who is constantly stumbling. If I am considered as a man who cannot be mistaken, then each of my mistakes must appear as a lie or a hypocrisy. But if I am regarded as a weak man, I appear then what I am in reality : a pitiable creature, yet sincere ; who has constantly and with all his soul desired, and who still desires, to become a good man, a good servant of God."

Thus he remained, tormented by remorse, pursued by the mute reproaches of disciples more energetic and less human than himself ;[1] tortured by his weakness and indecision, torn between the love of his family and the love of God—until the day when a sudden fit of despair, and perhaps the fever which rises at the approach of death, drove him forth from the shelter of his house, out upon the

---

[1] It seems that during his last few years, and especially during the last few months, he was influenced by Vladimir-Grigorovitch Tchertkoff, a devoted friend, who, long established in England, had consecrated his fortune to the publication and distribution of Tolstoy's complete works. Tchertkoff had been violently attacked by Leo, Tolstoy's eldest son. But although he was accused of being a rebellious and unmanageable spirit, no one could doubt his absolute devotion ; and without approving of the almost inhuman harshness of certain actions apparently committed under his inspiration (such as the will by which Tolstoy deprived his wife of all property in his writings without exception, including his private correspondence), we are forced to believe that he thought more of Tolstoy's fame than Tolstoy himself.

roads, wandering, fleeing, knocking at the doors of a convent, then resuming his flight, and at last falling upon the way, in an obscure little village, never to rise again.[1] On his death-bed he wept, not for himself, but for the unhappy ; and he said, in the midst of his sobs :

" There are millions of human beings on earth who are suffering: why do you think only of me ? "

Then it came—it was Sunday, November 20, 1910, a little after six in the morning—the " deliverance," as he named it : " Death, blessed Death."

[1] The *Correspondance* of the *Union pour la Verité* publishes, in its issue for January 1, 1911, an interesting account of this flight.

Tolstoy left Yasnaya Polyana suddenly on October 28, 1910 (November 10th European style) about five o'clock in the morning. He was accompanied by Dr. Makovitski ; his daughter Alexandra, whom Tchertkoff calls " his most intimate collaborator," was in the secret. At six in the evening of the same day he reached the monastery of Optina, one of the most celebrated sanctuaries of Russia, which he had often visited in pilgrimage. He passed the night there ; the next morning he wrote a long article on the death penalty. On the evening of October 29th (November 11th) he went to the monastery of Chamordino, where his sister Marie was a nun. He dined with her, and spoke of how he would have wished to pass the end of his life at Optina, " performing the humblest tasks, on condition that he was not forced to go to church." He slept at Chamordino, and next morning took a walk through the neighbouring village, where he thought of taking a lodging ; returning to his sister in the afternoon. At five o'clock his daughter Alexandra unexpectedly arrived. She doubtless told him that his retreat was known, and that he was being followed ; they left at once in the night. " Tolstoy, Alexandra, and Makoviktsi were making for the Koselk station, probably intending to gain the southern provinces, or perhaps the Doukhobor colonies in the Caucasus." On the way Tolstoy fell ill at the railway-station of Astapovo and was forced to take to his bed. It was there that he died.

XVIII

CONCLUSION

XVIII

THE struggle was ended ; the struggle that had lasted for eighty-two years, whose battlefield was this life of ours. A tragic and glorious mellay, in which all the forces of life took part ; all the vices and all the virtues.—All the vices excepting one : untruth, which he pursued incessantly, tracking it into its last resort and refuge.

In the beginning intoxicated liberty, the conflict of passions in the stormy darkness, illuminated from time to time by dazzling flashes of light— crises of love and ecstasy and visions of the Eternal. Years of the Caucasus, of Sebastopol ; years of tumultuous and restless youth. Then the great peace of the first years of marriage. The happiness of love, of art, of nature—*War and Peace*. The broad daylight of genius, which bathed the whole human horizon, and the spectacle of those struggles which for the soul of the artist were already things of the past. He dominated them, was master of them, and already they were not enough. Like Prince Andrei, his eyes were turned towards the vast skies which shone above the battlefield. It was this sky that attracted him :

"There are men with powerful wings whom pleasure leads to alight in the midst of the crowd, when their pinions are broken ; such, for instance, am I. Then they beat their broken wings ; they launch themselves desperately, but fall anew. The wings will mend. I shall fly high. May God help me !"[1]

These words were written in the midst of a terrible spiritual tempest, of which the *Confessions* are the memory and echo. More than once was Tolstoy thrown to earth, his pinions shattered. But he always persevered. He started afresh. We see him hovering in "the vast, profound heavens," with his two great wings, of which one is reason and the other faith. But he does not find the peace he looked for. Heaven is not without us, but within us. Tolstoy fills it with the tempest of his passions. There he perceives the apostles of renunciation, and he brings to renunciation the same

---

[1] *Journal*, dated October 28, 1879. Here is the entire passage :

"There are in this world heavy folk, without wings. They struggle down below. There are strong men among them : as Napoleon. He leaves terrible traces among humanity. He sows discord.—There are men who let their wings grow, slowly launch themselves, and hover : the monks. There are light fliers, who easily mount and fall : the worthy idealists. There are men with powerful wings. . . . There are the celestial ones, who out of their love of men descend to earth and fold their wings, and teach others how to fly. Then, when they are no longer needed, they re-ascend : as did Christ."

ardour that he brought to life. But it is always
life that he strains to him, with the violence of a
lover. He is "maddened with life." He is "intoxicated with life." He cannot live without this madness.[1] He is drunk at once with happiness and
with unhappiness, with death and with immortality.[2]
His renunciation of individual life is only a cry of
exalted passion towards the eternal life. The peace
which he finds, the peace of the soul which he
invokes, is not the peace of death. It is rather the
calm of those burning worlds which sail by the
forces of gravity through the infinite spaces. With
him anger is calm,[3] and the calm is blazing. Faith
has given him new weapons with which to wage,
even more implacably, unceasing war upon the lies
of modern society. He no longer confines himself
to a few types of romance ; he attacks all the great
idols : the hypocrisies of religion, the State, science,
art, liberalism, socialism, popular education, bene-

[1] "One can live only while one is drunken with life
(*Confessions*, 1879). "I am mad with living. . . . It is summer,
the delicious summer. This year I have struggled for a long
time ; but the beauty of nature has conquered me. I rejoice
in life." (Letter to Fet, July, 1880.) These lines were written
at the height of the religious crisis.

[2] In his *Journal*, dated May 1, 1863 : "The thought of
death." . . . "I desire and love immortality."

[3] "I was intoxicated with that boiling anger and indignation which I love to feel, which I excite even when I feel it
naturally, because it acts upon me in such a way as to calm
me, and gives me, at least for a few moments, an extraordinary
elasticity, and the full fire and energy of all the physical and
moral capacities." (*Diary of Prince D. Nekhludov*, Lucerne,
1857.)

volence, pacificism.[1]   He strikes at all, delivers his
desperate attacks upon all.

From time to time the world has sight of these
great rebellious spirits, who, like John the Forerunner, hurl anathemas against a corrupted civilisation.   The last of these was Rousseau.   By his love
of nature,[2] by his hatred of modern society, by his

---

[1] His article on *War*, written on the occasion of the
Universal Peace Congress in London in 1891, is a rude satire
on the peacemakers who believe in international arbitration :
" This is the story of the bird which is caught after a pinch
of salt has been put on his tail.   It is quite as easy to catch
him without it.   They laugh at us who speak of arbitration
and disarmament by consent of the Powers.   Mere verbiage,
this !   Naturally the Governments approve : worthy apostles !
They know very well that their approval will never prevent
their doing as they will." (*Cruel Pleasures.*)

[2] Nature was always "the best friend" of Tolstoy, as he
loved to say : "A friend is good ; but he will die, or he will
go abroad, and one cannot follow him ; while Nature, to which
one may be united by an act of purchase or by inheritance, is
better.   Nature to me is cold and exacting, repulses me and
hinders me ; yet Nature is a friend whom we keep until death,
and into whom we shall enter when we die." (Letter to Fet,
May 19, 1861.   *Further Letters.*)   He shared in the life of
nature ; he was born again in the spring.   " March and April
are my best months for work."   Towards the end of autumn
he became more torpid.   " To me it is the most dead of all
the seasons ; I do not think ; I do not write ; I feel agreeably
stupid." (To Fet, October, 1869.)   But the Nature that spoke
so intimately to his heart was that of his own home, Yasnaya
Polyana.   Although he wrote some very charming notes upon
the Lake of Geneva when travelling in Switzerland, and
especially on the Clarens district, whither the memory of
Rousseau attracted him, he felt himself a stranger amid the
Swiss landscape ; and the ties of his native land appeared
more closely drawn and sweeter : "I love Nature when she

jealous independence, by his fervent adoration of the Gospel and for Christian morals, Rousseau is a precursor of Tolstoy, who says of him :

"Pages like this go to my heart ; I feel that I should have written them." [1]

surrounds me on every side, when on every hand the warm air envelopes me which extends through the infinite distance ; when the very same lush grasses that I have crushed in throwing myself on the ground make the verdure of the infinite meadows ; when the same leaves which, shaken by the wind, throw the shadow on my face, make the sombre blue of the distant forest ; when the very air I breathe makes the light-blue background of the infinite sky ; when not I alone am delighting in nature ; when around me whirl and hum millions of insects and the birds are singing. The greatest delight in nature is when I feel myself making a part of all. Here (in Switzerland) the infinite distance is beautiful, but I have nothing in common with it." (May, 1851.)

[1] Conversations with M. Paul Boyer (*Le Temps*, August 28, 1901).

The similarity is really very striking at times, and might well deceive one. Take the profession of faith of the dying Julie :

"I could not say that I believed what it was impossible for me to believe, and I have always believed what I said I believed. This was as much as rested with me."

Compare Tolstoy's letter to the Holy Synod :

"It may be that my beliefs are embarrassing or displeasing. It is not within my power to change them, just as it is not in my power to change my body. I cannot believe anything but what I believe, at this hour when I am preparing to return to that God from whom I came."

Or this passage from the *Réponse à Christophe de Beaumont*, which seems pure Tolstoy :

"I am a disciple of Jesus Christ. My Master has told me that he who loves his brother accomplishes the law."

Or again :

"The whole of the Lord's Prayer is expressed in these

But what a difference between the two minds, and how much more purely Christian is Tolstoy's ! What a lack of humility, what Pharisee-like arrogance, in this insolent cry from the *Confessions* of the Genevese :

" Eternal Being ! Let a single man tell me, if he dare : I was better than that man ! "

Or in this defiance of the world :

" I say it loudly and fearlessly : whosoever could believe me a dishonest man is himself a man to be suppressed."

Tolstoy wept tears of blood over the " crimes " of his past life :

" I suffer the pangs of hell. I recall all my past baseness, and these memories do not leave me ; they poison my life. Usually men regret that they cannot remember after death. What happiness if

words : 'Thy Will be done !'" (*Troisième lettre de la Montagne.*)

Compare with :

"I am replacing all my prayers with the *Pater Noster*. All the requests I can make of God are expressed with greater moral elevation by these words : 'Thy Will be done !'" (Tolstoy's *Journal*, in the Caucasus, 1852–3.)

The similarity of thought is no less striking in the province of art :

"The first rule of the art of writing," said Rousseau, "is to speak plainly and to express one's thought exactly."

And Tolstoy :

"Think what you will, but in such a manner that every word may be understood by all. One cannot write anything bad in perfectly plain language."

I have demonstrated elsewhere that the satirical descriptions of the Paris Opera in the *Nouvelle Héloise* have much in common with Tolstoy's criticisms in *What is Art?*

it should be so ! What suffering it would mean if, in that other life, I were to recall all the evil I have done down here ! " [1]

Tolstoy was not the man to write his confessions, as did Rousseau, because, as the latter said, "feeling that the good exceeded the evil it was in my interest to tell everything." [2] Tolstoy, after having made the attempt, decided not to write his *Memoirs;* the pen fell from his hands ; he did not wish to be an object of offence and scandal to those who would read it.

"People would say : There, then, is the man whom many set so high ! And what a shameful fellow he was ! Then with us mere mortals it is God who ordains us to be shameful." [3]

Never did Rousseau know the Christian faith, the fine modesty, and the humility that produced the ineffable candour of the aged Tolstoy. Behind Rousseau we see the Rome of Calvin. In Tolstoy we see the pilgrims, the innocents, whose tears and naïve confessions had touched him as a child.

But beyond and above the struggle with the world, which was common to him and to Rousseau, another kind of warfare filled the last thirty years of Tolstoy's life ; a magnificent warfare between the highest powers of his mind : Truth and Love.

Truth—"that look which goes straight to the heart," the penetrating light of "those grey eyes which pierce you through "—Truth was his earliest faith, and the empress of his art.

[1] *Journal,* January 6, 1903.   [2] *Quatrième Promenade.*
[3] Letter to Birukov.

" The heroine of my writings, she whom I love with all the forces of my being, she who always was, is, and will be beautiful, is Truth." [1]

The truth alone escaped shipwreck after the death of his brother.[2] The truth, the pivot of his life, the rock in the midst of an ocean.

But very soon the "horrible truth"[3] was no longer enough for him. Love had supplanted it. It was the living spring of his childhood ; "the natural state of his soul."[4] When the moral crisis of 1880 came he never relinquished the truth ; he made way for love.[5]

Love is "the basis of energy."[6] Love is the "reason of life ; the only reason, with beauty."[7] Love is the essence of Tolstoy ripened by life, of the author of *War and Peace* and the *Letter to the Holy Synod.*[8]

[1] *Sebastopol in May, 1853.*

[2] " The truth. . . . the only thing that has been left me of my moral conceptions, the sole thing that I shall still fulfil." (October 17, 1860.)

[3] *Ibid.*

[4] " The love of men is the natural state of the soul, and we do not observe it." (*Journal,* while he was a student at Kazan.)

[5] " The truth will make way for love." (*Confessions.*)

[6] " ' You are always talking of energy ? But the basis of energy is love,' said Anna, ' and love does not come at will.' " (*Anna Karenin.*)

[7] " Beauty and love, those two sole reasons for human existence." (*War and Peace.*)

[8] " I believe in God, who for me is Love." (*To the Holy Synod,* 1901.)

" ' Yes, love ! . . . Not selfish love, but love as I knew it, for the first time in my life, when I saw my enemy dying at my

This interpenetration of the truth by love makes the unique value of the masterpieces he wrote in the middle part of his life—*nel mezzo del cammin*—and distinguishes his realism from the realism of Flaubert. The latter places his faith in refraining from loving his characters. Great as he may be, he lacks the *Fiat lux !* The light of the sun is not enough : we must have the light of the heart. The realism of Tolstoy is incarnate in each of his creatures, and seeing them with their own eyes he finds in the vilest reasons for loving them and for making us feel the chain of brotherhood which unites us to all.[1] By love he penetrates to the roots of life.

But this union is a difficult one to maintain. There are hours in which the spectacle of life and its suffering are so bitter that they appear an affront to love, and in order to save it, and to save his faith, a man must withdraw to such a height above the world that faith is in danger of losing truth as well. What shall he do, moreover, who has received at the hands of fate the fatal, magnificent gift of seeing the truth—the gift of being unable to escape from seeing it ? Who shall say what Tolstoy suffered from the continual

side, and loved him. . . . It is the very essence of the soul. To love his neighbour, to love his enemies, to love all and each, is to love God in all His manifestations ! . . . To love a creature who is dear to us is human love : to love an enemy is almost divine love !'" (Prince Andrei in *War and Peace.*)

[1] "The passionate love of the artist for his subject is the soul of art. Without love no work of art is possible." (Letter of September, 1889.)

discord of his latter years—the discord between his unpitying vision, which saw the horror of reality, and his impassioned heart, which continued to expect love and to affirm it ?

We have all known these tragic conflicts. How often have we had to face the alternative—not to see, or to hate ! And how often does an artist— an artist worthy of the name, a writer who knows the terrible, magnificent power of the written word—feel himself weighed down by anguish as he writes the truth ! [1] This truth, sane and virile, necessary in the midst of modern lies, this vital truth seems to him as the air we breathe . . . But then we perceive that this air is more than the lungs of many can bear. It is too strong for the many beings enfeebled by civilisation ; too strong for those who are weak simply in the kindness of their hearts. Are we to take no account of this, and plunge them implacably into the truth that kills them ? Is there not above all a truth which, as Tolstoy says, "is open to love" ? Or is the artist to soothe mankind with consoling lies, as Peer Gynt, with his tales, soothes his old dying mother ? Society is always face to face with this dilemma : the truth, or love. It resolves it in general by sacrificing both.

Tolstoy has never betrayed either of his two faiths. In the works of his maturity love is the torch of truth. In the works of his later years

---

[1] "I write books, which is why I know all the evil they do." . . . (Letter to P. V. Veriguin, leader of the Doukhobors, 1898. *Further Letters.*)

it is a light shining on high, a ray of mercy
which falls upon life, but does not mingle with
it. We have seen this in *Resurrection*, wherein
faith dominates the reality, but remains external
to it. The people, whom Tolstoy depicts as
commonplace and mean when he regards the
isolated figures that compose it, takes on a divine
sanctity so soon as he considers it in the abstract.[1]

In his everyday life appears the same discord as
in his art, but the contrast is even more cruel.
It was in vain that he knew what love required
of him; he acted otherwise; he lived not according to God but according to the world. And
love itself: how was he to behave with regard to
love? How distinguish between its many aspects,
its contradictory orders? Was love of family to
come first, or love of all humanity? To his last
day he was perplexed by these alternatives.

What was the solution? He did not find it.
Let us leave the self-sufficient, the coldly intellectual, to judge him with disdain. They, to be
sure, have found the truth; they hold it with
assurance. For them, Tolstoy was a sentimen-
talist, a weakling, who could only be of use as a
warning. Certainly he is not an example that

---

[1] See the *Russian Proprietor*, or see in *Confessions*, the
strongly idealised view of these men, simple, good, content
with their lot, living serenely and having the sense of life:
or, at the end of the second part of *Resurrection*, that vision
"of a new humanity, a new world," which appeared to
Nekhludov when he met the workers returning from their
toil.

they can follow : they are not sufficiently alive.
Tolstoy did not belong to the self-satisfied elect ;
he was of no Church ; of no sect ; he was no
more a Scribe, to borrow his terms, than a Pharisee
of this faith or that. He was the highest type of
the free Christian, who strives all his life long
towards an ideal that is always more remote.[1]

Tolstoy does not speak to the privileged, the
enfranchised of the world of thought ; he speaks
to ordinary men—*hominibus bonae voluntatis.* He
is our conscience. He says what we all think,
we average people, and what we all fear to read
in ourselves. He is not a master full of pride :
one of those haughty geniuses who are throned
above humanity upon their art and their intelligence. He is—as he loved to style himself in
his letters, by that most beautiful of titles, the
most pleasant of all—" our brother."

[1] " A Christian should not think whether he is morally
superior or inferior to others ; but he is the better Christian
as he travels more rapidly along the road to perfection,
whatever may be his position upon it at any particular
moment. Thus the stationary virtue of the Pharisee is less
Christian than that of the thief, whose soul is moving rapidly
towards the ideal, and who repents upon his cross." (*Cruel
Pleasures.*)

INDEX

INDEX

(The names of characters and titles of books are in italics).

ALEXANDRA, Tolstoy's aunt, 18
Ancestry, Tolstoy's, 14, 15
Analysis, self-, 29
Andrei Bolkonsky, Prince, 88–90
  94, 100
Anna Karenin (novel), 76, 84,
  99, 102, 203
Anna Karenin (character), 103,
  104
Arabian Nights, 19, 169
Art—
  Attacks on modern, 145, 146
  Tolstoy's conception of, 147–
    150
  His ignorance of, 151
  His religious ideal of art, 156
  Christian art extinct, 157
  The art of the future, 159
  Endowment of, 159
  Mission of, 160
Austerlitz, 89, 90

BACH, 153
Bachkirs, the, 102
Bagration, 88
Beethoven, 151, 155, 181, 183
Bers family, the, 75
Bers, S. A., 179

Bers, Sophie, *see* Countess
  Tolstoy
Besoukhov, Pierre, 88, 91–4,
  100
Bloody Sunday, 212
Böcklin, 151
Boyer, Paul, 167
Boyhood, 42
Brahms, 151
Breton, Jules, 151
Brothers, Tolstoy's, 17
Brush with the Enemy, A, 44
Bylines, 19, 168

CAUCASUS, Tolstoy joins Army
  of the, 33
Census, the, Tolstoy assists in
  taking, 127
Chavannes, P. de, 151
Childhood, Tolstoy's, 17–19
Childhood, Boyhood, Youth, 15,
  16, 19, 23
  Begun in the Caucasus, 35 ; 39
  Tolstoy's later opinion of, 40 ;
    84
  See *Boyhood* and *Youth*
China, Tolstoy's admiration for,
  220

Christ, Tolstoy's conception of, 119

Concordance and Translation of the Four Gospels, 118

Confessions, 106, 120, 238

Cossacks, The, 44

Countess Tolstoy—
Character and abilities, 83
As model, 84; 100, 135–8, 226–7
Letter to, 229–31

Creed, Tolstoy's, 123–4

Crimea, transference to the, 49

Criticism of Dogmatic Theology, 118

Criticism of art, destructive, 151

Cycle of Readings, 200

DEATH OF IVAN ILYITCH, THE, 6, 68, 165, 174–5

Decembrists, The (a projected novel), 91

Diary of a Sportsman, 68, 75

Diary of Prince D. Nekhludov, 65

Dmitri Tolstoy, 17
Death of, 106–7

Don Quixote, 158

Dostoyevsky, 158, 193

Dreyfus Affair, the, 154

Droujinine, 61

EDUCATION, Tolstoy's ideas concerning, 23–5, 66

End of a World, The, 201

England, Tolstoy contemplates retiring to, 103

Erochta, the old Cossack, 45

Execution, effect of a public 64

FAITH, Tolstoy's, brings no happiness, 128

Family, Tolstoy's, 16

Family dissensions, 228

Family Happiness, 75–7, 84

Father, Tolstoy's, 16

Feminism, Tolstoy's attitude towards, 138

Flaubert's opinion of Tolstoy's work, 99, 245

GAPON, FATHER, 212

George, Henry, 225

Georgians, the, 213

Goethe, 156

Gontcharev, 61

Great Crime, The, 201, 210

Greek, Tolstoy studies, 101

Gricha, the idiot, 18

Grigorovitch, 61

HADJI MOURAD, 199

Hebrew, Tolstoy studies, 137

Home, Tolstoy's, *see* Yasnaya Polyana

Hugo, Victor, 158

Hunting, renounced, 132

IBSEN, 151

Introspection, Tolstoy's faculty of, 29

Invasion, The, 35, 42

Irtenieff, Nikolas, 15

JOSEPH, the History of, 19, 159

Journal, Tolstoy's, 14, 27, 34

KARENIN, 106
Karatayev, 91
Kazan, 23
Khlopoff, Captain, 43
Kitty Levine, 84, 103
Klinger, Max, 151
Kozeltoff, brothers, in *Sebastopol in August, 1855*, 56–7
Kreutzer Sonata, The, 165, 174, 176–7, 181
Kutuzof, 88, 90–1

LEVINE, 103, 106–8, 111
Lhermitte, 151
Liberal Party, Tolstoy's disdain of the, 66, 202–3
Life, 120
Literary Society of St. Petersburg, Tolstoy's dislike of, 61–67
Logic, heroic, 129–130
Love—
    Definition of, 122
    Tolstoy's attitude towards sexual, 177
    Law of, 211
Lucerne, incident of the singer, 65

MANET, 151
Marriage, Tolstoy's views concerning, 100, 177
Marie, Princess, 88–9
Marie Tolstoy, 16, 94
Maslova, 191
Master and Servant, 165
Michelangelo, 151
Millet, 151

Molière, 158
Moscow, effect of visit to, 127, 130, 147
Music—
    Love of, 28–9
    Ignorance of modern music, 151–2 ; 153
    In the *Kreutzer Sonata*, 178
    Dread of, 179
    Suggested State control over, 182–3

NATASHA, 90, 93–4, 179–180
Nekhludov, 26–8, 33, 68, 181, 191
Nekhludov, Diary of Prince D., 65
Nikolas Tolstoy, 17, 33
    Dies of phthisis, 69
Non-Resistance, 211, 225

OLD BELIEVERS, the, 212
Olenin, 45
Orthodox Church, Tolstoy's relations with the, 117
Ostrovsky, 61

PAKHOM THE PEASANT, 169-170
Parents, Tolstoy's, 15–16
Pascal, 120
Pedagogy, 135
Polikushka, 70, 78
Popular Tales, 42, 165, 168
Popular idiom, 167–8
Portraits of Tolstoy—
    Of 1848, 26 (note)
    Of 1851, 35
    Of 1856, 61
    Of 1885, 129 ; 140

Posdnicheff, 177, 182
Power of Darkness, The, 165, 170-3
Prashkhoukhine, death of, 54

REASON (letter upon), 121
Reason, Tolstoy's distrust of, 108 ; 120-121
Religion—
  Tolstoy's vague agnosticism as a youth, 24
  Revival of, in the Caucasus, 33-9 ; 100, 123-4, 135, 209, 215-16
Rembrandt, 151
Resurrection, 166, 187-195, 224, 247
Revolution, Tolstoy prophesies, 209-10
Roumania, Tolstoy joins Army of, 49
Rousseau, J. J., worship of, 27 ; 240-3
Rules of Life, 25
Russian Proprietor, A, 27
  Written in the Caucasus, 35 ; 42
Russo-Japanese War, 201

ST. PETERSBURG, Tolstoy's dislike of literary society of, 61, 67
Samara, 192
Schopenhauer, 101 (note)
Science, Tolstoy attacks, 145
Sebastopol in December, 1854, 52
Sebastopol in May, 1855, 52-6

Sebastopol in August, 1855, 52, 54-7
Sebastopol, the siege of, 49-57
Sexual morality, 177
Shakespeare, 166
Shakespeare, no artist, 152-3, 155-6
Siegfried, hasty judgment on, 152
" Smartness," Tolstoy's worship of, 27
Socialism, Tolstoy's hatred of, 205-8
Society, pictures of Russian, 103
Sophia Bers, *see* Countess Tolstoy
Sovremennik, the (Russian review), 40
Spelling-book, Tolstoy's, 135
State, the, a murderous entity, 130
Stepan Arcadievitch, 105
Sterne, influence of, 41
Story-teller, a blind, 19
Strauss, 151
Stuck, 151
Suarès, 6, 61
Suicidal tendencies, 107, 111, 113

TATIANA, Tolstoy's aunt, 17
Tchaikowsky, 151
Terror, attack of nervous, 100
Three Deaths, 68
Three Old Men, 168
Tolstoy, Countess, 75, 83, 84, 100, 135-8, 226-7, 229-231

Tolstoy, Dmitri, 17
  Death of, 106–7
Tolstoy, Leo—
  Reception of his work in France, 6
  Influence of Rousseau and Stendhal, 7
  Organic unity of his life, 13
  Ancestry and inheritances, 14–15
  Childhood, 17–19
  Student days, 23–5
  Personal appearance (see Portraits), 25–6
  Joins Army of Caucasus, 33
  Religious experiences, 33–4
  First literary work, 35
  Effects of illness, 39
  Early work, 41–5
  Love of life, 46
  Transferred to Crimea, 49
  Narratives of Sebastopol, 52
  Enters St. Petersburg literary society, 61
  Quarrels with Tourgenev, 63
  Travels in Europe, 64
  Studies pedagogy, 66
  Effect of his brother's death, 70
  Courtship, 75
  Marriage, 76–83
  War and Peace, 83–95
  Anna Karenina, 99
  Effect of Dmitri's death, 107
  Suicidal tendencies, 111
  His " conversion," 115–16
  Joins the Orthodox Church, 117

Tolstoy Leo (*continued*)—
  Leaves it, 117
  Visits Moscow, 127
  Commences to write on religious subjects, 136
  Differences with Countess Tolstoy, 136–7
  Spiritual loneliness, 140
  Attacks upon modern art and science, 145
  His ignorance of art, 151
  Ignorance of modern music, 152
  Attack upon Shakespeare, 153–7
  Religious and æsthetic ideals, 156–61
  His fear of music, 178–80
  Political ideals, 214
  Religious ideals, 215–16
  Old age, 219
  Political hopes, 220
  Loneliness, 228
  Intends leaving his family, 229
  Death, 234
Tolstoy, Nikolas, 17, 33, 69
Töppfer, influence of, 41
Tourgenev, 17, 61–3
  Criticism of Tolstoy, 95, 140, 202
Turkey, war declared upon, 49
Two Hussars, The, 68

VOLODYA, see *Kozeltoff*
Vogüé, Melchior de, 140
Vronsky, 103–4

WAGNER, Tolstoy's hasty judgment of, 152, 155
War and Peace, 15, 43, 84, 95, 99–101, 103–5
What I Believe, 141
What is Art? 149–50, 166
What shall we do? 129, 138
Woman, Tolstoy's ideal of, 138–9

Woodcutters, The, 44

YASNAYA POLYANA, 16, 33
Tolstoy returns to, 65
Experiments at, 66–7; 224, 228
Youth —
Written during the siege of Sebastopol, 50
Lyrical beauty of, 51

107547

LIBRARY
OF
MOUNT ST. MARY'S
COLLEGE
EMMITSBURG, MARYLAND